MESSAGE OF THE FATHERS OF THE CHURCH

General Editor: Thomas Halton

Volume 16

MESSAGE OF THE FATHERS OF THE CHURCH

PRAYER

Personal and Liturgical

by

Agnes Cunningham, S.S.C.M.

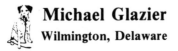 **Michael Glazier**
Wilmington, Delaware

ABOUT THE AUTHOR

Agnes Cunningham, S.S.C.M., theologian and patristic scholar, is Professor of Patrology and Director of the Department of Church History at Saint Mary of the Lake Seminary in Mundelein, Illinois. She is past president of the Catholic Theological Society of America (1977-1978), and is currently on the Board of Directors of Sacred Heart School of Theology (Hales Corners, Wisconsin) and of *Contemplative Review.* She is theological consultant to the NCCB Ad Hoc Committee on Women in Society and the Church. Among her recent publications is *The Bishop in the Church: Patristic Texts on the Role of the* Episkopos.

First published by 1985 Michael Glazier, Inc. 1723 Delaware Avenue, Wilmington Delaware 19806

Distributed outside U. S., Canada, Australia, and Philippines by Geoffrey Chapman, a division of Cassel Ltd., 1 Vincent Square, London SWIP 2PN.

Library of Congress Catalog Card Number: 84-48852
International Standard Book Number:
  Message of the Fathers of the Church series:
    (0-89453-312-6, Paper, 0-89453-340-1, Cloth)
  PRAYER
    0-89453-327-4

Cover design: Lillian Brulc

Printed in the United States of America

*IN MEMORY of my parents
Monica and Michael
who first taught me that prayer is
a matter of mind and heart,
of soul and strength, and of loving service
to the poor and needy*

Acknowledgements

Several people have to be recognized for their assistance in the completion of this volume. In the first place, I am grateful to those students at Saint Mary of the Lake Seminary in Mundelein, Illinois who allowed me to pursue the basic research for this work in several research seminars in the Canonical Degree Program, while they were working on theses projects. Their insights and challenges are reflected in the final material and its presentation. Two co-workers, especially, deserve a particular word of thanks: Mrs. Gloria Sieben, Head Librarian at Saint Mary of the Lake Seminary, whose competence and encouragement were a constant inspiration and a gentle goad; Lynne Godwin, my everfaithful, diligent and optimistic secretary who never ceased to assure me that the task would, indeed, arrive at completion.

To Michael Glazier, for the initial invitation and the never failing patience he has extended to me, sincere and warm thanks, too!

CONTENTS

Part I

The Patristic Doctrine of Christian Prayer

Part II

Selections From the Writings of the Fathers

EDITOR'S INTRODUCTION

The *Message of the Fathers of the Church* is a companion series to the *Old Testament Message* and the *New Testament Message*. It was conceived and planned in the belief that Scripture and Tradition worked hand in hand in the formation of the thought, life and worship of the primitive Church. Such a series, it was felt, would be a most effective way of opening up what has become virtually a closed book to present-day readers, and might serve to stimulate a revival in interest in Patristic studies in step with the recent, gratifying resurgence in Scriptural studies.

The term "Fathers" is usually reserved for Christian writers marked by orthodoxy of doctrine, holiness of life, ecclesiastical approval and antiquity. "Antiquity" is generally understood to include writers down to Gregory the Great (+604) or Isidore of Seville (+636) in the West, and John Damascene (+749) in the East. In the present series, however, greater elasticity has been encouraged, and quotations from writers not noted for orthodoxy will sometimes be included in order to illustrate the evolution of the Message on particular doctrinal matters. Likewise, writers later than the mid-eighth century will sometimes be used to illustrate the continuity of tradition on matters like sacramental theology or liturgical practice.

An earnest attempt was made to select collaborators on a broad inter-disciplinary and inter-confessional basis, the chief consideration being to match scholars who could handle the Fathers in their original languages with subjects in which they had already demonstrated a special interest and competence. About the only editorial directive given to the selected contributors was that the Fathers, for the most part, should be allowed to speak for themselves and that they should speak in readable, reliable modern English. Volumes on individual themes were considered more suitable than volumes devoted to individual Fathers, each theme, hopefully, contributing an important segment to the total mosaic of the Early Church, one, holy, catholic and apostolic. Each volume has an introductory essay outlining the historical and theological development of the theme, with the body of the work mainly occupied with liberal citations from the Fathers in modern English translation and a minimum of linking commentary. Short lists of Suggested Further Readings are included; but dense, scholarly footnotes were actively discouraged on the pragmatic grounds that such scholarly shorthand has other outlets and tends to lose all but the most relentlessly esoteric reader in a semi-popular series.

At the outset of his *Against Heresies* Irenaeus of Lyons warns his readers "not to expect from me any display of rhetoric, which I have never learned, or any excellence of composition, which I have never practised, or any beauty or persuasiveness of style, to which I make no pretensions." Similarly, modest disclaimers can be found in many of the Greek and Latin Fathers and all too often, unfortunately, they have been taken at their word by an uninterested world. In fact, however, they were often highly educated products of the best rhetorical schools of their day in the Roman Empire, and what they have to say is often as much a lesson in literary and cultural, as well as in spiritual, edification.

St. Augustine, in *The City of God* (19.7), has interesting reflections on the need for a common language in an expanding world community; without a common language a man is more at home with his dog than with a foreigner as far as intercommunication goes, even in the Roman Empire, which imposes on the nations it conquers the yoke of both law and language with a resultant abundance of interpreters. It is hoped that in the present world of continuing language barriers the contributors to this series will prove opportune intepreters of the perennial Christian message.

Thomas Halton

Introduction

From the earliest ages of Christianity, the followers of Jesus have sought to respond to his teachings and his mandates, in fidelity to a gospel that proclaims a universal call to holiness (cf. Vatican II, *Lumen gentium*, chapter V). In terms of prayer, this response has had to include the courage to grapple with a doctrine that admonishes believers to "keep on praying and never lose heart" (Lk 18:1)[1] and the creativity to probe the meaning of an injunction to confide one's entire life and all one's concerns to the God who is Father (cf. Lk 11:1-2).

The revival of interest in patristic studies, especially since Vatican II, provides the context within which we can go to the men and women of the age known as Christian Antiquity to hear what they have to say about Christian prayer, both personal and liturgical. We are not the first generation of disciples to seek the counsel of the Fathers on the question of prayer. The teaching that comes to us from the first centuries of the Christian era has inspired and funded the heritage of Christian spirituality throughout the centuries. Our particular interest, at this time, is born of the conviction that only by standing on the shoulders of the giants of the past[2] can we hope to see more clearly the panoramic horizons of the Kingdom of God that lie before our eyes.

[1] All scriptural quotations are from the New English Bible.

[2] This phrase is frequently used to refer to the recourse later ages have had to the Fathers.

1. The Nine Ways of Prayer of St. Dominic

Some months ago, I came upon an illustrated version of Saint Dominic's "nine ways of praying": inclinations, genuflections, prostrations, penance, contemplation, earnest intercession, supplication, thoughtful reading, and praying on a journey.

> [This] way of praying [is one] in which the soul uses the members of the body in order to rise more devotedly to God, so that the soul, as it causes the body to move, is in turn moved by the body, until sometimes it comes to be in ecstasy like Paul, sometimes in agony like our Saviour, and sometimes in rapture like the prophet David.[3]

In studying and reflecting on the small figure who demonstrates the saint's teaching, I have come to realize that Dominic stands firmly in the tradition of the great teachers and masters of prayer in the early Church. In fact, the document describing the nine ways begins with a recognition of the contribution of "Augustine, Leo, Ambrose, Gregory, Hilary, Isidore, John Chrysostom and John Damascene as teachers" of prayer. They held a concept that we could call, today, "wholistic prayer." Their prayer, like their love, was a response to the gospel imperative: "Love the Lord your God with all your heart, with all your soul, with all your strength, and with all your mind; and your neighbor as yourself" (Lk 10:27).

2. General Plan

In this volume, we intend to hear and examine a "message" from several Fathers (and from at least one "Mother") on prayer, personal and liturgical. In order to do this, we shall review early definitions and forms of prayer and shall

[3]"The Nine Ways of Prayer of St. Dominic" (trans., Simon Tugwell, O.P.). *Canadian Catholic Review*, March, 1983. P. 22/93.

attempt to formulate a theology of prayer in the light of available evidences from the first eight hundred years of the Christian era. Selections from specific documents will be presented in an attempt to demonstrate as complete a picture as possible of the way in which early Christians learned to pray and contributed to a developing understanding of prayer. In conclusion, a brief bibliography for further reading will be suggested. Perhaps the overall aim of this entire volume can be expressed in the words of one of the great early masters of prayer:

> *He prays without ceasing* who joins prayer to works that are of obligation and good works to his prayer. For virtuous works, or the carrying out of what is enjoined, form part of prayer. It is only in this way that we can understand the injunction, *pray without ceasing*, as something that we can carry out; that is to say, if we regard the whole life of the saint as one great continuous prayer.[4]

[4]*On Prayer*, Origen (trans., John J. O'Meara). ACW 19. Westminster, Maryland: The Newman Press, 1954. pp. 46-47.

Part I
The Patristic Doctrine of
Christian Prayer

Abbreviations

ACW   Ancient Christian Writers

CCL   Corpus Christianorum, series latiná

CSEL Corpus Scriptorum Ecclesiasticorum Latinorum

FOTC Fathers of the Church

GCS   Die Griechischen Christlichen Schriftsteller

LCL   Loeb Classical Library

SC   Sources chrétiennes

Chapter One

The Definition of Christian Prayer

It is a self-evident fact that prayer did not begin with Christianity. The early Christians inherited a strong and diversified tradition of prayer from Judaism, on the one hand, and an intense, if at times ambiguous, experience of pagan, Gentile prayer, on the other. Furthermore, once Christians began to pray *as Christians,* they did not immediately proceed to a definition of prayer. Indeed, they prayed, spoke and wrote about prayer long before they attempted to "define" it.

In the *Summa Theologica* (II-IIae, q. 83, a. 1), St. Thomas Aquinas presents several ancient Christian answers to the question, "What is prayer?" Augustine writes that, "prayer is a petition."[5] The same concept is expressed also by John Chrysostom:

> Think what happiness is granted you, what honor is bestowed on you, when you converse with God in prayer. Then, you speak with Christ, asking for whatever you will and for whatever you desire.[6]

Both Cassiodorus and John Damascene describe prayer in similar phrases. For Cassiodorus, "prayer (*oratio*) is spoken reason (*oris ratio*);"[7] for John Damascene, "to pray

[5] *De Verbi Domini.*
[6] *Homilies on Genesis* XIII, XXX. SC 7 (my translation). *On Prayer,* 2.
[7] *Commentary* on Psalm 38, 13.

17

is to ask becoming things of God."[8] Between the earliest expressions of a prayer that can be identified as Christian and more refined definitions of it, a long road has been traveled. That distance is not to be measured so much in time as in the Christian experience of faith and in the efforts to articulate that faith as it seeks understanding (*fides quaerens intellectum*).

The most helpful way in which to arrive at a "patristic definition of prayer" is to realize that the statement we seek will be *progressively theological.* Furthermore, in the earliest documents available to us, concepts of prayer will have to be derived from the prayer itself, rather than from descriptive statements about prayer. Thus, the *Didaché* (8, 2) gives this admonition: "*do not pray as the hypocrites do*, but pray as the Lord has commanded in the Gospel."[9] Clement of Rome writes: "Let us...fall on our knees before the Master, and with tears implore Him to have mercy on us. ...Let us...ask pardon for our waywardness....Let us ...pray for those who are guilty of some fault, that meekness and humility may be granted them....[10]

1. Selected Writers

The earliest examples of Christian prayer as well as the documents which provide directives for its expression clearly reflect the influence of Judaism and the Synagogue. A striking departure from this is found in Tertullian's treatise, *On Prayer* (*De Oratione*), in which he writes, "the prayer formulated by Christ consists of three elements: the spirit whereby it can have such power, the word by which it is expressed, and the reason why it produces reconciliation."[11] Tertullian insists that, with Christ, a new type of

[8] *De fide orthodoxa* III, 24.

[9] *The Didaché* ACW6, 1948, 19 (trans., James A. Kleist, S.J., Ph.D.).

[10] *Epistle to the Corinthians* (trans., James A. Kleist, S.J., Ph.D.). ACWI. Westminster, Maryland: The Newman Bookshop, 1946. pp. 39, 40, 43.

[11] *Prayer* (trans., Sister Emily Joseph Daly, C.S.J., Ph.D.). FOTC 40, 1959. 158.

prayer has been inaugurated. This prayer belongs, specifically, to the Christian. It is exemplified most clearly in the Lord's Prayer.

Origen, writing less than fifty years after Tertullian, has left us the oldest scientific discussion of Christian prayer in existence. The Alexandrian, drawing on the First Epistle to Timothy, uses four words for four realities that relate to the question of prayer: supplications, prayers, intercessions and thanksgivings. He then proceeds to explain these terms:

> ...*Supplication* is offered by one who needs something ...; *Prayer* is offered in conjunction with praise of God by one who asks in a more solemn manner for greater things; *Intercession* is the request to God...made by one who has greater confidence; and *Thanksgiving* is the prayer with acknowledgement to God for the favours received from God...[12]

2. Progressive Theological Intuitions

With Origen, then, a precise vocabulary entered into Christian Greek reflection on prayer: *deēsis* (supplication), *proseuchai* (prayer), *enteuxeis* (intercessions), *eucharistia* (thanksgiving). Further, he distinguished the prayer accompanied by vow (*euchē*) from the invocation (*proseuchē*) offered to God. At still another stage, Origen sought to order his vocabulary to progressive phases of prayer. Thus, *deēsis* (supplication) became the petition for spiritual, but limited, goods; *proseukē* (prayer) referred to one's self-abandonment to pure intercourse with God; *doxologia* (praise) was the prayer of total absorption in the glorification of God; *enteuxis* (intercession) was intercession for others. Finally, he concludes his treatise by a review of the "essential parts of prayer": *doxologia* (praise or glorification of God); *eucharistia* (thanksgiving); *exomologesis* (confession of sin); *aitesis* (petition).

[12] *On Prayer*, chapter 14, 2.

The development of thought that can be found in Origen's treatise is somewhat indicative of the progressive understanding and articulation of concepts of prayer expressed by later writers in the patristic era. Not all of these writers followed Origen's teaching in its entirety. However, as we examine his treatise on prayer, we can recognize the Alexandrian's influence both in the foundational principles and in the idea of developmental stages that have characterized the classic doctrines of prayer in the history of Christian spirituality.

Chapter Two

The Prayer of Christians

Tertullian insisted that in Jesus Christ, a new kind of prayer had been given to humanity. This prayer was to be found most clearly exemplified in the formula known as the Lord's Prayer. The significance of this prayer was marked by the place assigned to it in the eucharistic celebration from earliest times and by the attention given it in treatises and commentaries during the patristic age. Christian prayer, both personal and corporate, was shaped by the Lord's Prayer which provided a model for the Christian's approach to God and the parameters of the concerns to be embraced by the followers of Jesus. More basically, the importance of the preservation and "tradition" of the Lord's Prayer came

> from an understanding that one of the fundamental elements of Christian initiation in the catechumenate was a progressive introduction to Christian prayer, insofar as it is, specifically, a "filial prayer."[13]

Christians, therefore, prayed as Jesus had prayed and as Jesus had taught them to pray. The Lord's Prayer quickly acquired a normative value. For both Jewish and pagan

[13]I have borrowed this thought from the description of a course in Liturgy to be offered by Irénée-Henri Dalmais, as described in the 1982-83 catalog of the Institut Catholique, Paris. My translation.

converts seeking to address the Christian God in an appropriate manner, a structure and words were available. More than that, there was an implicit, formative pedagogy that descibed the boundaries to which Christian prayer might extend and inspired the boundless confidence with which every concern could be entrusted to God's love and mercy.

1. Personal Prayer and Communal Prayer

Although the personal prayers of an individual carried a certain priority over public worship at one point, the early Church was conscious of having inherited a regular pattern of formal prayer from Jesus. Before the end of the second century, daily prayer was offered at morning, noon, evening and midnight. Nonetheless, liturgical prayer and personal prayer appear together in some confusion throughout the early ante-Nicene period, while persecuted Christians sought in the forms and usages of Judaism the means to express the intensity of their spiritual enthusiasm and their conviction of an imminent *eschaton*.

2. Liturgical Prayer and Eucharist

Throughout the first three centuries, the heart of all Christian prayer was the celebration of the Eucharist. In this action, believers, then, and we, still today, offer to God only that which God has first given us and that gift which is useless to One who has need of nothing. Nonetheless, this is the "spotless offering" in every place (cf. Mal 1:11) by which the Church continues to be reborn, even as she faithfully does what the Lord first did.

Before Justin (*Apology* I, 65-67), we do not find any texts that give us both a description of the celebration of the Eucharist and an explanation of the deep meaning which Christians discerned in the eucharistic offering. This is true despite the eucharistic references in earlier documents such as Clement's *First Letter to the Corinthians* (40:1-5; 41:1-2) with its anaphora-like prayer of thanksgiving (59:2—61:3); the images that run like an organ-point through the letters of Ignatius of Antioch; the Christian dimensions that enhance the basic Jewish format of the invocations of the *Didaché* (9, 10, 14).

For Christians of the pre-Nicene era, the whole of their participation in the eucharistic liturgy was symbolized in their AMEN. In a later age, Augustine was to find the words to express this earlier intuition:

> If you are the Body and members of Christ, it is the sacrament of your very self that is placed on the Lord's table; it is the sacrament of your very self that you receive. You answer 'Amen' to what you are; and this answer is a recognition. You hear said, The 'Body of Christ'. Be a *real* member of Christ's Body so that your 'Amen' will be the truth.[14]

At times, celebration of the Eucharist was frequent and ordinary. Jerome writes of a bishop whose love for poverty left him with only a wicker basket to hold the body of the Lord and a plain glass cup to contain the precious blood.[15] At other times, the eucharistic liturgy was more formal, even splendid. This was, especially, the situation following the peace of Constantine when a strong impetus was given to the official prayer of the Church, the liturgy. Daily as well as Sunday celebration became the norm. Matins and Vespers were recited in the cathedral church on a daily basis. By the end of the fourth century, precise regulations concerning the *Horae* could be found in the *Apostolic Constitutions*.

Despite a progressive tendency toward the establishment of standardized rulings for Christian liturgical prayer, a great deal of variety and diversity continued to persist

[14]Sermon 272, PL 38: 1247-1248. Cited in, *The Church and Christian Prayer*. Hervé Savon. Saint Severin Series for Adult Christians III. Notre Dame, Indiana: Fides Publications, Inc., 1965. p. 53. (English version by Geoffrey Stevens).

[15]Letter CXXV, 20, "To Rusticus."

throughout the Church. This diversity was reflected, above all, in the multiple modes and observances that character-ized and revealed the manner in which Christians prayed, alone and together.

Chapter Three

Forms of Prayer

1. Kinds of Prayer

In considering the diversity that marked Christian prayer in the age of the Fathers, we can examine, briefly, the kinds and modes of prayer and the recorded observances that were, in themselves, understood to be prayer.

The term, *kinds* of prayer, refers to the different types of prayer which individual Christians chose in their approach to God and in their conversation with the Deity. We have already found an identification of the basic types of prayer in Origen. Within the boundaries established by Christian revelation and the order of salvation, the followers of Jesus prayed as they lived: as citizens of two worlds. Reflection on this twofold experience resulted in what might be called an "existential" prayer.[16] Primary concerns were the daily confession of faith in a spirit of eschatological readiness for the Second Coming or for martyrdom and of intercession for the needs of the Church and the world.

As the Alexandrians, Clement and Origen, were to explain, this vocal prayer would become purified and interiorized to go

> beyond itself into the prayer of silence, characterizing the state of union with God in a liberation from the body.

[16] *La Prière II: Les trois premiers siècles.* A. Hamman, O.F.M. Tournai (Belgium): Desclée et Cie, Editeurs, 1963. p. 5.

> Then prayer becomes vision, but it is a vision of
> love....[17]

The mystical dimension of prayer perceived by these earlier Fathers was to be the focus of later teaching in the patristic age. Thus, Augustine thought that prayer enables us to relive "that crossing into the spiritual world which we have already experienced in a mysterious and hidden way in baptism."[18] The efforts of Christians in the third century to foster prayer through the wedding of personal piety and some type of "doctrinal architecture"[19] were realized, to some extent, with the rise of monasticism. The Jesus-Prayer, the use of Scripture interspersed with psalmody to encourage lengthy "ruminations" on the revealed text, the "pure prayer" of Evagrius: all were meant to facilitate obedience to the Lord's injunction to pray ceaselessly, a "goal towards which all the efforts of the monk are to be oriented."[20]

2. Modes of Prayer

The *modes* or formal structures of Christian prayer developed, in great part, out of monasticism, as this institution became a charismatic factor of renewal in the Church. In this renewal, Christians were called back to remember the roots and sources from which their communal prayer had originally sprung: meditation on the passion of Christ and on the Cross which, without the *corpus*, was a sign of victory (*tropaion*) in the early Church; reading of the Holy Scriptures as spiritual nourishment; asceticism, that *sine qua non* of a prayer that penetrates and transforms the whole of life.

---

[17]*The Spirituality of the New Testament and the Fathers, Louis Bouyer.* (trans., Mary P. Ryan). History of Christian Spirituality I. New York/Tournai/Paris/Rome: Desclée and Company, Inc., 1963. p. 299.

[18]Savon, *op. cit.* p. 61.

[19]Hamman, *op. cit.* p. 7.

[20]Bouyer, *op. cit.* p. 529.

Under the rubric of "modes" of prayer can be considered gestures and movements such as those included by St. Dominic in his nine ways of praying. The words of Psalm 84 came to life in early Christian prayer: "my whole being cries out with joy to the living God." Prayers were to be offered standing, except during times of penance or penitence. Christians were to face towards the East when they prayed. The Church at prayer was symbolized in the figure of the *Orans*, a woman standing with arms outstretched and palms raised to heaven. When asked, "how should one pray?" Macarius was to answer: "It is enough to hold out one's hands and to say: Lord, as You know and will; have mercy" (*Apophthegm* 16). Deep inclinations from the waist and prostrations also had their time and place. The "prayer of the hands" and of the whole body gave outer accord to the inner concentration of one's thoughts on Christ.

With all of this, the practice of liturgical prayer, even as it developed structurally, preserved distinctive customs from one local Church or region to another. From the synagogue-like gatherings where Christians first assembled for readings and intercessions, the eucharistic supper enshrined in Prayer and Word became the focus of all Christian worship and the central experience of Christian spirituality.

3. Observances

In complementarity to an increasingly contemplative personal prayer and a progressively structured liturgical prayer, a number of *observances* were also recognized in the early Church as expressions of prayer and communion with God and as attempts to sanctify time and space through the saving grace of Christ.

In this category, we can consider, first of all, the observance of the Lord's day, the "day of the Sun," as Justin phrased it. Abandonment of the Jewish Sabbath was one of the deliberate choices made to establish a uniquely Christian identity. Closely associated with this observance was the celebration of the Lord's Resurrection: on every Sunday, in some places; on the fourteenth day of Nisan, in those churches influenced by the Jerusalem tradition; on the first Sunday following the first full moon, after the Spring equinox, in churches which adopted the Roman practice. This diversity was to reach a point of crisis on two occasions, prompting the intervention, first, of Polycarp of Smyrna and, later, of Irenaeus of Lyons in the Quartodeciman controversy.

Still other "observances" counted as prayer included fasting on Wednesday and Friday until 3:00 P.M., an hour chosen to coincide with the time of Christ's death. Other forms of asceticism included freely chosen austerity of life, manual labor — particularly in the monasteries, pilgrimages to shrines and holy places, a spirit of poverty and humility in following the Christian life.

The two most honored "observances" were almsgiving and the faithful witness of martyrdom. Cyprian called "barren" (*sterilis oratio*) a prayer which did not "go hand in hand with alms." Origen considered martyrdom the crowning perfection of a prayer that had penetrated and transformed a Christian's entire life at the price of a "crucifying asceticism." Both of these observances were celebrated around the eucharistic table, where a martyr's relics became a source of inspiration and courage and where the offerings of the assembly were entrusted to their president for distribution to the needy.

Our efforts to arrive at an understanding of the prayer of the early Church depend, to a great extent, on our ability to retrieve the multiple ways in which Christians prayed through kinds, modes and observances such as those described above. It is also necessary to attempt to discern in these diverse manners of praying the underlying teachings that emerged in that era from the Fathers who have left us the basic elements of a doctrine of prayer and the foundations for a theology of prayer.

Chapter Four

Toward a Theology of Prayer in the Fathers

A review of the teachings of the Fathers on prayer leads to a recognition of the developmental character of those teachings. Early understandings of Christian prayer were progressively theological and increasingly wholistic or integrated. These qualities apply to personal, individual prayer as well as to group or corporate prayer, whether that was charismatic or liturgical in nature. Observances that emerged, gradually, throughout the patristic age were also marked by an underlying theological intuition that pointed to the desire to embrace the whole of life and, in the case of the early martyrs, that moment of life that was their death.

While it may not be possible to articulate a formal, systematic "theology of prayer" in the patristic era, it is not difficult to identify the elements that characterize a general doctrine of Christian prayer in that age. These elements can be considered under the headings of *mission, mysticism* and *memorial.*

1. Mission

The concept of Church as *missio*, as it has been articulated since Vatican II, is not native to the period of Christian Antiquity. However, as early as Clement of Rome and the years of *ad intra* concerns in the Church, we find an awareness of the Christian's responsibility to pray for the State, for the temporal rulers of the empire, and for the Lord's disciples as they lived out their duties as citizens of this world.

What theologians today call "contextualization" constituted the ambiance within which Christians lived, prayed, suffered and died. Christians were men and women of the time in which they lived. The externals of daily life in the Roman mode impinged on the worship of the Church and on the manner in which Christian prayer enabled the followers of the Lord to respond in collaboration or resistance to the ideology and the *mores* of society.

Diversity of culture throughout the empire was another aspect of contextualization which came to bear on the development of Christian prayer in its various kinds, modes and observances. From the situation of Clement, writing to the Corinthians from the heart and capitol of the empire as the voice of the "Church residing as a stranger at Rome" to the personalized reflections of a fifth-century lady-pilgrim, Egeria, the prayer of the Church was the prayer of an *ecclesia* in mission: concerned that others hear the Good News, come to know the Lord Jesus, choose to commit their lives to him in faith, love and service.

2. Mysticism

The age of the Fathers of the Church is not, ordinarily, associated with the rise of mysticism or with mystical prayer. However, a history of mysticism that omits or underestimates the contribution that emerges in the patristic era has to be incomplete and lacking in one of its foundation stones.

The roots of mystical prayer can be most readily discovered in the exultant exclamations of Ignatius of Antioch and in his soaring apostrophes and acclamations. The vision and enthusiasm of Ignatius carry a certain contagion for holy things, for heavenly spheres, for the desire to "be dissolved and to be with Christ." In the Ignatius *corpus*, we find the seeds of that experience of contemplation that appears again and again in the history of Christian prayer —from Clement of Alexandria and Origen to Augustine; from the early poets and hymnodists to the reflections of Dionysius the Areopagite; from every attempt to probe the simplicity of the Lord's Prayer to ecstatic penetration of the mysteries represented in murals, frescoes and ikons.

3. Memorial

Christians prayed *in memory of* Christ. Early prayers were addressed to the Father *in remembrance of* his "beloved Child, Christ Jesus." The memorial *par excellence*, however, was the eucharistic celebration. In the prayer of the Eucharist, every type, form and observance of prayer was echoed or symbolized. The memorial of the eucharistic prayer was the prayer of Christ and the prayer of the Church. It was sacrament and sacramental. In the Eucharist, the mighty deeds of God proclaimed by Abraham, Isaac and Jacob, by Moses and the prophets, were hailed as the heritage of the new Israel. In the Eucharist, the promises of God in Christ were recalled in anticipation of an imminent Second Coming. In the Eucharist, the body of Christ was "re-membered" in his Church.

As we read the messages concerning prayer, as these are transmitted to us in the writings of the Fathers of the Church, a pattern begins to emerge. Out of this pattern, we can move toward a tentative articulation of an early theological understanding of Christian prayer as an activity by which a disciple of the Lord, with him and through him, seeks God in faith, intercedes with God in hope, experiences and communes with God in love and, fiiled with the Spirit of Jesus, reaches out in concern and service to others. In other words, Christian prayer, as understood and taught by the Fathers, was, essentially, christological — therefore, biblical and ecclesiological — therefore, sacramental. These elements have been preserved in the best traditions of Christian spirituality, throughout the ages. There is every reason for us to find ourselves at home with the Fathers in prayer.

Part II
Selections from the Writings of the Fathers

The following selections from the writings of the Fathers have been chosen for their representativity of the scope, the depth, and the quality of a patristic doctrine of prayer. Many other texts might have been taken, in place of those included in this volume. Indeed, other publications, such as A. Hamman's, *Early Christian Prayer* (Chicago: Henry Regnery Company, 1961), contain a rich and varied collection of prayers from the early Church.

Both unity and diversity mark the kinds of prayer presented here. The selections date from the late first to the fifth century of the Christian era. They were authored by martyrs, bishops and theologians; by a poet, a missionary, a philosopher and a mystic. Until relatively recently, one author has been suspect of heresy. Another died a schismatic. Each of them has contributed in a unique and positive manner to the development of a tradition of prayer and spirituality to which we can turn, today, for inspiration and education.

Chapter Five

Christian Prayer Before Nicaea

In the period prior to the Council of Nicaea (A.D. 325), Christian prayer tended to follow the patterns inherited from Judaism. Not only were prayers expressed in the vocabulary and symbols of the Old Testament. The internal and external structures of prayer, for example, the times and postures of prayer, were freely borrowed from the rituals of the synagogue.

Christian prayer came to be *Christian* in the ante-Nicene period because of Christian faith in Jesus as Lord and in the God revealed by Jesus as well as because of the Christian experience of martyrdom.

1. Clement of Rome

Clement, bishop of Rome, is generally recognized as the earliest known Father of the Church and the first of the Apostolic Fathers. The years of his leadership of the Church at Rome are usually accepted as A.D.92-A.D. 101, although some authors, by way of exception, submit an earlier date. The *First Epistle to the Corinthians*, his only certainly authentic, known work was written in the name of the Church of Rome to the Christians of Corinth, on the occasion of a crisis resulting from the unorthodox rejection of validly-appointed leaders of the Church at Corinth.

The letter contains an intercessory prayer (59, 2-62; 64) that reflects the general concerns of the Christian community, a particular concern for those involved in the turmoil and unrest at Corinth, and the earliest known Christian petition for civil rulers. In the prayer we find echoes of both Judaic vocabulary and the Christian liturgy, as it was celebrated at Rome.

59[21]   With prayers and supplications, let us earnestly entreat the Creator of the universe to preserve the whole and entire the designated number of his elect throughout the entire world, for the sake of his beloved child, Jesus Christ, our Lord. Through him, we have been called from darkness to light, from ignorance to the knowledge of the glory of his Name.

Thus, we are able, also, to hope in your Name, from which every creature has its origin.

You have opened the eyes of our heart, so that we may know you, who alone are the Most High in the heights of heaven, the Holy One among the saints.

You confound the arrogance of the haughty; bring to nothing the schemes of the nations; raise up the lowly and humble the proud; enrich and improverish; take life away and bestow it.

You are the sole benefactor of the human mind and the God of all flesh.

You sound the deepest recesses and survey the actions of human beings.

You are the helper of all who are in danger and the saviour of the hopeless.

You are the creator and the *episkopos* of all spirits.

You multiply the nations of the earth and from among them you have chosen, through Jesus Christ your beloved child, those who love you. Through this same Lord you have instructed, sanctified and honored us.

We beseech you then, Master, to be our helper and our

---

[21]Greek text: (SC 167).

protector. Save all of us who are in tribulation, uplift all who have fallen, be near to those in need; heal the sick, lead back those who have wandered far from your flock; feed the hungry, liberate those who have been taken captive from out of our midst. Strengthen the weak, confirm the cowardly. Let all nations know that you are the only God, that Jesus Christ is your child, and that "we are your people and the sheep of your pasture."

Indeed, you have made visible the eternal, dynamic, sustaining order of the world. Lord, you have created the earth. In every generation, you are the Faithful One, judging justly, admirable in magnificence and strength. In wisdom, you have created every living being; with understanding, you sustain them all. You are the goodness of all visible things, full of kindness to all who hope in you, merciful and compassionate. Forgive the sins and injustices, the faults and failings of which we are guilty. Do not consider the sin of your servants and handmaidens, but cleanse us with the purifying action of your truth. Direct our feet, so that we may walk in holiness of heart, doing all that is good and pleasing in your eyes and in the eyes of those who rule us. Yes, Master, let your face shine on us to confirm us in peace; save us from your mighty hand and deliver us from all sin through your exalted arm; rescue us from all who hate us unjustly. Grant tranquility and peace to us and to all the inhabitants of the earth, as you have already given peace to our ancestors when they called upon you faithfully in truth and holiness. Help us to obey your omnipotent and excellent Name and to be submissive to our leaders and governors on this earth.

Master, you have bestowed on them the power of royalty by your magnificent, ineffable might so that we might recognize the glory and honor you have given them and be submissive to them, according to your will. Lord, grant them health, peace, harmony, and stability, so that they might exercise the sovereignty you have entrusted to them, free from constraint. For it is you, heavenly ruler, king of the ages, who grant glory, honor and power over earthly things to the children of mankind. Lord, direct their decisions towards goodness and what is acceptable in your sight. May they exercise with piety, in peace and meekness, the power you have given them and thus find favor before you. We give thanks to you who alone can fulfill these requests and even greater benefits to us. We offer gratitude to you through the high priest and protector of our souls, Jesus Christ. Through him be glory and honor to you, now and from generation to generation and for all the ages to come. Amen.

2. *Ignatius of Antioch*

Ignatius, bishop of Antioch in Syria, suffered martyrdom about the year A.D. 110. The *corpus* of seven letters, written on his way to Rome as a prisoner, reflects the heart and mind of one who could, without embarrassment, call himself, "*Theophoros*," "God-bearer."

The following selection is a composite of excerpts taken from his epistle to the Ephesians, written during a brief stay at Smyrna, en route to the capital of the empire (II, 2; III, 1; IV, 2; IX; X; XI; XXI).[22]

It is right to glorify Jesus Christ in every way; he has glorified you. I am not giving you an order, as if I were important. For, even if I am in chains for the sake of the Name, I have not yet grown to full stature in Jesus Christ. Only now am I beginning to be his pupil and I speak to you as fellow disciples. I need to be anointed by your faith, your exhortations, your patience and your forbearance. Each one of you, together, ought to form a chorus, so that in harmonious consonance, taking in unity the note intoned by God, you may, as a single voice, sing a hymn to the Father, through Jesus Christ. So will he listen to you and recognize you, through the good works you do, as members of his Son. This is why it is important for you to be inseparable in your unity, so that you may always share in God, himself.

[22]Greek text: (SC 10)

You are stones for the Father's temple, hoisted on high by the crane of Jesus Christ, I mean, his cross, with the Holy Spirit acting as a cable for you. Your faith draws you up; love is the pathway by which you ascend toward God. Thus, all of you are, also, traveling companions, bearing God, bearing the temple, bearing Christ, bearing sacred vessels. In all things, you are adorned with the precepts of Jesus Christ.

Pray without ceasing for others. There is hope that they will repent and come to God. At least, let them become your disciples because of the works you do. When they are angry, be gentle and mild. When they boast and brag, be humble. When they blaspheme, pray. When they go astray, remain steadfast in faith. When they are brutal, be a peacemaker. Do not seek to become like them. Let us be brothers and sisters to them, showing goodness to them, as we strive to be imitators of the Lord. Who among us has been the object of most injustice? Who has been the most deprived? Who, most rejected? Let not one of the devil's weeds grow up in your midst. In all purity and temperance may you abide, body and spirit, in Jesus Christ. Only if we are found to be in Christ will we enter into true life. Have no treasures apart from him. It is in him that I wear these chains as spiritual pearls. Would that I might rise, still wearing them, because of your prayer. In that prayer I hope always to share, as an heir of the Christians in Ephesus, who have always remained united to the Apostles, through the power of Jesus Christ.

Remember me, as Jesus Christ is mindful of you. Pray for the Church in Syria. Keep well in God the Father and in Jesus Christ, who is the hope we share in common.

3. Polycarp of Smyrna

As a grown man, the great Irenaeus, second-century bishop of Lugdunum (Lyons) in the Roman province of Gallia (Gaul), remembered vividly the instructions he

had received as a child from "the blessed Polycarp" who,
himself, had listened to John and "the rest of those who
had seen the Lord." After eighty-six years of fidelity in the
service of Christ, Polycarp was apprehended, tried and
condemned to death. Christians hailed him as "an apostolic and prophetic teacher"; pagans recognize him as
"the teacher of Asia, the father of the Christians, the
destroyer of our gods."

The *Martyrdom of Polycarp* is an eyewitness account
that reveals, through the story of one individual, the
theological and spiritual understanding of martyrdom in
the early Church. In the following excerpts from this
document (5, 7, 8, 14, 15, 19),[23] we are given a portrait of
the bishop of Smyrna as a man of prayer.

The most admirable of the martyrs was Polycarp. First of
all, when he learned all that had taken place, he was not
upset. He even wanted to stay in town. Because everyone
insisted, however, he agreed to leave. He took refuge on a
small piece of property not far from the city, where he stayed
with a few companions. Night and day he did nothing but
pray for all people and for all the churches throughout the
world. This was what he always did. During prayer, he had a
vision in which he saw his pillow on fire. Going to his
companions, he said to them: "I am going to be burned
alive."

(Apprehended by the imperial soldiers, Polycarp asks for
time to pray, before being taken to prison)

He asked only that he be granted one hour in which he
might pray freely. His request was granted and, standing, he
began to pray aloud, like one who has been filled with the
grace of God. And so he prayed aloud for two hours, unable
to stop. Those who heard him were overcome with amaze-
ment. Many of the soldiers were filled with regret for having

[23]Translated and slightly adapted from the French text in *L'Empire et La Croix*,
Adalbert Hamman, O.F.M., éditeur. Lettres Chrétiennes, 2. Paris: Grasset, Edi-
tions de Paris, 1957. (Greek text of Funk-Bihlmeyer consulted in *Sources Chrétiennes* 10a)

come out against so holy an old man.

Then, he finished his prayer, in which he had remembered everyone he had known during the course of his long life: the little ones and the great; the noble and the lowly and the entire catholic Church spread throughout the whole world. The hour for his departure came. It was the great Sabbath day.

(The moment comes for Polycarp to be burned at the stake.)

Bound to the stake, with his hands fastened behind his back, Polycarp seemed like a choice ram, selected from an entire flock and readied for sacrifice. Lifting his eyes to heaven, he prayed:

> "Lord, Almighty God, Father of Jesus Christ, your blest and well-loved child, through whom we have come to know you; God of angels and celestial powers; God of all creation and of the entire family of the just who live in your presence: I bless you for having judged me worthy to come to this day and this hour. You have counted me worthy to stand among the number of your martyrs and to share the chalice of your Christ, so that I might rise to eternal life, soul and body, in the incorruptibility of the Holy Spirit.
>
> May I be received with them, today, in your presence as a precious and welcome oblation. You have prepared me for this; you have foretold me of this. You have kept your promise, O faithful God, God of Truth. For this grace and for everything you have given me, I praise you and bless you. I glorify you through Jesus Christ, the eternal and heavenly High Priest, your beloved Child.
> Through him who is with you and the Spirit may glory be given, now and for all the ages to come. Amen."

When Polycarp had finished his prayer and pronounced this "Amen," the fire was lit and the flame leaped up, high and burning. It seemed to form an arch or a sail, filled with wind, and embraced the martyr's body. The bishop stood in the midst of the fire not like burning flesh, but like bread turning golden as it bakes, or like silver and gold refined in a crucible.

That is the story of blessed Polycarp. Now he is with the Apostles and all the just, joyfully glorifying God the Father almighty and blessing our Lord Jesus Christ, the Savior of our souls, the Master of our bodies, the Shepherd and Pastor of the catholic Church, spread throughout the entire world.

4. The Christian Martyrs of Gaul

In the year A.D. 177, the Christian community of Vienne and Lyon (LUGDUNUM) was subjected to a violent persecution in which the elderly bishop, Pothinus, was put to death along with a great number of the faithful. One of the most extraordinary witnesses was given by the slave-girl, Blandine, whose faith and courage sustained others in their trials and earned for her the title, "mother" of the martyrs.

The account of this persecution is recorded in a letter to the Christians of Asia and Phrygia under the title, "Acts of the Martyrs of Lyon." The author of the letter is unknown.[24]

(Following the apprehension, trial and condemnation of the Christians, some of them are brought before the crowd in the arena.)

Indeed, all of us were concerned about Blandine, as was her mistress who was also among the martyrs in this struggle. This lady doubted that Blandine could confess her faith with conviction because of her physical weakness. But Blandine, on the contrary, was imbued with such strength that she exhausted and eliminated from the contest the train of executioners who succeeded one another in torturing her

[24]Eusebius, HE v. 1.3-2.8 (Schwartz. 402.ff).

from morning to night. They, themselves, admitted they were vanquished, with nothing else left that they could do to her. It was they who were astonished to see breath still left in her body, torn and stabbed as it was. They affirmed that one type of torture alone should have been enough to kill her. There ought not to have been so many of them making such great efforts. The blessed young woman, however, like a courageous athlete, felt renewed and restored by her confession of faith. She found consolation, calm and a kind of medicinal relief from her sufferings in the words, "I am a Christian and there is nothing evil that occurs among us." (Several Christians are publicly tortured and put to death. Blandine is then led out into the arena for her first combat.)

As for Blandine, she was hung to a stake, that day, and set out as fodder for the beasts released about her. Seeing her fastened, as it were, to a cross and hearing her praying aloud, her two companions found consolation and strength. In the midst of their struggles, their eyes, fixed on their sister, beheld him who had been crucified for them: Christ. They looked on him who had suffered death on a cross in order to assure those who believe in him that whoever suffers for the glory of Christ enters into communion with the living God forever. Not one of the beasts touched Blandine, that day. She was taken down from the stake and led back into prison, to be kept for a new combat. Thus, victorious after a series of trials, she was to reverse the chastisement of the insidious Serpent. She was to become a living sermon for her brothers, small, weak and despised as she was, but shielded as if by armor, by Christ, himself, the great, invincible Athlete. In many encounters with the Demon, she was the conqueror and at the battle's end received the crown of immortality.

(After all her companions had been put to death, Blandine is led out to be the last martyr.)

The blessed Blandine remained last of all. She was like a mother whose great heart has found the way to support her children by her own words and to encourage them to go forward unconquered toward God. Then, in her turn, she endured all the sufferings to which her children had been subjected. Filled with joy and gladness as she neared the end, she hastened to join those who had gone before her, as if she were preparing for a wedding banquet and not for an encounter with wild beasts. Whips, animals and gridiron were employed in succession. Then, at the end, she was enclosed in a net to be thrown before a wild bull. As she was tossed repeatedly into the air by the animal, she lost all sense of what was happening to her, so intent was she on those blessings for which she hoped, in faith; so captivated was she by her communion with Christ. She, too, was immolated, at last. The pagans, themselves, acknowledged that they had never seen a woman suffer such great and so many torments.

Chapter Six

The Lord's Prayer

Throughout the history of Christianity, saints and scholars have sought to probe the deep meaning of the prayer which Jesus taught his followers. In every age, the petitions of The Lord's Prayer have been sounded in search of a resonance that echoes the concerns and needs of a new generation. Believers continue to hope to find through these inspired words light and strength to live the gospel, in fidelity to the past and with creativity for the future.

In the following selections, a choice has been made of five commentaries on the same petitions "Our Father, who art in heaven"; "Thy will be done on earth as it is in heaven"; "Lead us not into temptation but deliver us from evil." in the prayer taught by Jesus to his disciples. In comparing these five commentaries on the Lord's Prayer from the patristic age, we can discover signs of development in scriptural interpretation, in doctrinal articulation and in pastoral concern. In these texts, we have a model for contemporary reflections on this essentially Christian prayer.

1. Tertullian

Between the years A.D. 200 and A.D. 206, Tertullian, "the first true Western theologian," as Cayré calls him, wrote a treatise on prayer (*De oratione*). This work begins with a detailed explanation of each petition of the Lord's Prayer. Written in the early period following Tertullian's conversion from paganism to Christianity, the *De oratione* reflects some of the best spiritual teaching bequeathed to us by this frequently impassioned and increasingly heterodox author.

There are several points to be noticed about Tertullian's treatment of the petition, "Thy will be done..." In Tertullian's text, this phrase comes immediately after "Hallowed be thy name." Scholars do not agree on the reason for this. Perhaps Tertullian was familiar with a version of the prayer circulating in northern Africa, at that time. Perhaps he followed what he perceived to be a more logical sequence in the phrases. Secondly, we note an inversion within the phrase as we know it today. Tertullian places "in heaven" before "on earth." Here, again, no conclusive explanation has been offered by scholars for this.

On another point, Tertullian refers to a possible literal ("straightforward") understanding of the petition. This is a curious reference, especially since Tertullian is usually looked upon by contemporary biblical scholars as a "sober exegete." Furthermore, the symbolic or allegorical method of scriptural exegesis was developed in Alexandria, not in northern Africa (Carthage), where Tertullian lived. Once again, we encounter paradox in this, perhaps, most paradoxical of the Ante-Nicene Christian writers.

Finally, the relationship of the meaning of this particular petition to the sufferings of Christ, as indicated by Tertullian, reminds us of the importance he attributed to this dimension of the Christian life. As he was drawn to Christianity by the patient endurance of the martyrs under persecution and torture, so he was, eventually, persuaded to abandon a Church in which extreme asceticism had given way, in his eyes, to laxity. Fortunately, none of that later exaggeration can be found in his treatise on prayer.

1.[25] The prayer begins with a confession of belief in God and a merit-bearing act of faith, as we say, "Father, who art in heaven." For this form of address results when we adore God and affirm our faith. It is written, "To those who believe in God, he gave the power to be called children of God." Our Lord often spoke to us of God as a Father. Indeed, he taught us to call no one on earth "father," but the one who is Father in heaven. Thus, when we pray in this manner, we are also obedient to the Lord's precept. Happy are they who know their Father! The Spirit calls heaven and earth as witnesses, when the reproach is brought against Israel, "I have begotten sons who have not known me." Further, when we say, "Father," we add a title to God's name, too. That name expresses both filial love and power. Again, when we invoke the Father, the Son, also, is addressed. For Christ said, "I and the Father are one." Moreover, our Mother the Church is not neglected, for the Mother is recognized in the Son and in the Father; the words "Father" and "Son" depend on her for their meaning. Thus, with this one term or word, we honor God together with those who are his own, we obey his precept and we admonish those who do not recognize who their Father is.

4. Following this, we add: *thy will be done in heaven and on earth.* We are not praying because someone actually could prevent the accomplishment of God's will or as if our prayers could assure its fulfillment. Rather, we pray for God's will to be done in everyone. Through symbolic interpretation, we understand that we, flesh and spirit, are heaven and earth. If, however, we are to take these words straightforwardly, the sense of this petition is the same: that the will of God may be done in us, on earth, certainly so that it may also be done in the same way, in heaven. Now, what does God will more than that we walk along the way he has taught us? We ask, then, that the substance and the resources of his will be supplied to us, that we might be saved both in heaven and on earth. For the fullness of his will is that those he has adopted as children be saved.

[25]Latin text: CCL 1

The will of God was also fulfilled by the Lord in his preaching, his works and his sufferings. If he, himself, claimed that he came not to do his own, but the Father's will, surely, what he did was the will of the Father. We are called now to take his actions as a model, so that we, too, may preach, work and suffer, even unto death. If we are to be able to accomplish such things, God's will must be done.

Again, when we say, "*Thy will be done,*"we are wishing ourselves well, for there is no evil in the will of God, even though some penalty other than what one would desire be imposed on a person who deserves it.

By praying in this manner we further prepare ourselves to suffer patiently. Our Lord chose to reveal the weakness of the flesh when he felt the full burden of his passion. At that moment, he prayed: *Father, let this cup pass from me.* But he added, after pondering in his heart, "yet not my will, but thine be done." He was, himself, the will and the power of the Father. Still, he submitted fully to the Father's will, in order to manifest clearly that we also are to exercise patient endurance.

8. In order that this brief prayer might be complete in its arrangement, Christ added that we ought to pray not only that our sins be forgiven, but that we might totally avoid them. "Lead us not into temptation": in other words, do not let us be led astray by the Tempter. Let us not even think that the Lord appears to be the one who tempts us — as if he were not aware of the faith of an individual or, even, were bent on disturbing it! That kind of weakness and malice belongs to the devil. Even in the case of Abraham, God commanded the sacrifice of his son not to tempt his faith, but to prove it. In Abraham, God would set an example of that precept by which he was to teach, in time, that no one should love even his nearest and dearest more than God. Christ, himself, was tempted by the devil and unmasked for us that subtle master of temptation. He emphasizes this petition at a later time when he says, "Pray that you enter not into temptation." Still, they were tempted and deserted their Lord, falling asleep rather than persevering in prayer. Thus, the last phrase of this petition balances the first and points to its

meaning: "Lead us not into temptation"; "but deliver us from evil."

2. Origen

In Part Two of his treatise, *On Prayer*, Origen presents his commentary on the Lord's Prayer. In his reflection on the third petition, he indicates briefly that Luke has omitted this phrase, which follows "Thy kingdom come," in the Matthean text. He chooses to follow Matthew.

Origen's commentary evidences that spiritual understanding of the Scriptures which particularly characterized the Alexandrian School. Every word and phrase is probed so that, beneath the "body" of the text, the "soul" and the "spirit" may be discovered.

As the "founder of biblical science" in the Christian tradition, Origen developed not only an exegetical methodology for the interpretation of Scripture, but also a theology of the written Word of God. Basic to his theological teaching is the understanding of a threefold sense in the Bible. 1) The corporal ("somatic") sense, founded on the text itself with its literal and historical data, constituted the "body" of Scripture. 2) The moral ("psychic") sense was the "soul." 3) The spiritual ("pneumatic") sense, the "spirit," provided a deeper meaning and the promise of heavenly goods to come.

It is not difficult to perceive the differences between this text below and that of Tertullian. In addition to the distinctive exegetical method, there are signs of a development in Christology, with echoes of Origen's *Logos* theology. Like the commentary from North Africa, this text speaks to us of an effort to respond to the needs of a specific Christian community, one marked, in this instance, by the diversity and culture of a great city.

Chapter 22.[26] 1. *Our Father who art in heaven.* It is indeed worth our while to examine with care the Old Testament, as

[26]Text: Koetschau, ed. GCS

it is called, to see if we can find it in any prayer offered by a person who calls God, "Father." Although we have examined that writing as carefully as possible, we have not so far found any such instance. Of course, this is not to say that God is not referred to as "Father." Nor do we imply that those who believed in God were not known as "sons of God." We, however, have yet to find in any prayer an expression of that trust, proclaimed by the Savior, which addresses God as "Father." We can find many places in the text where God is called "Father" and where those who invoke the Word of God are called "sons." For example, we read in Deuteronomy, "You have forsaken the God that begot you and have forgotten the God that nourished you." Again, "Is not he who possessed you, made you and created you, your father?" Further, ". . . sons that are unfaithful." In Isaiah, we find this: "I have brought up children; I have exalted them, but they have despised me." In Malachias, "The son shall honor the father and the servant, his master. If, then, I am a father, where is my honor? And if I am a master, where is the fear due to me?"

3. If we could understand what is implied by the words written in Luke, "When you pray, say, Father," we would shrink from using that name, unless we were true sons, lest impiety be added to our other sins. I am trying to express what Paul wrote in the First Epistle to the Corinthians, "No one can say, 'Lord Jesus,' except by the Holy Spirit" and "no one speaking by the Spirit of God says 'anathema' to Jesus." "Holy *Spirit*" and "Spirit of God" mean the same to him. Now, the meaning of the phrase, "to say 'Lord Jesus' by the Holy Spirit" is not exactly clear. Hypocrites beyond counting, many who are heterodox and even, at times, evil spirits who are conquered by the power of that Name invoke these words. No one will dare to argue that any such persons "say 'The Lord Jesus' by the Holy Spirit." Therefore, it cannot be shown that they say "Lord Jesus." Only those who are servants of the Word of God, those who in all they do call no one Lord but him, can say "Lord Jesus," just by their very being. If it is these who say, "Lord Jesus," then it is probable

also that everyone who sins cursed the Word of God by his sinning. His evil deeds cry out, "Anathema to Jesus." Since one kind of person says "Lord Jesus" and another, "Anathema to Jesus," so "whosoever is born of God" and refrains from sinning, participates in the seed of God which preserves him from all sin. Such a person's actions proclaim, "Our Father who art in Heaven." Thus, "the Spirit himself gives witness to their spirit" that they are "the children of God, heirs of God and co-heirs with Christ." As they suffer with him, they may also truly hope to be glorified together with him. So that such as these may not say "Our Father" only half-heartedly, their hearts must be united to their works. The heart, which is the source and origin of good works, must "believe unto justice," while "their mouth" in harmony "confesses unto salvation."

Chapter 26. 1. *Thy will be done on earth as it is in heaven.* Following "Thy kingdom come," Luke has omitted this petition and writes, "Give us each day our supersubstantial bread." Let us now consider the words which came next in order and which we have found only in Matthew. We who pray while we are still on earth must understand that the will of God is done in heaven by all who are there with God. Let us, then, pray that his will be done by us on earth, in all things, just as it is done by those who are in heaven. This will happen if we do nothing opposed to the will of God. When God's will is done on earth by us as it is in heaven, then shall we be like those who are in heaven: we, too, shall bear the image of the heavenly bodies; we shall be heirs to the kingdom of heaven. Those who come after us, while they are still on earth, will pray to be like us, for we shall then be in heaven.

3. Someone reading these words, *Thy will be done on earth as it is in heaven*, might ask: How can the will of God be done in heaven where there are superhuman powers of evil which require that the sword of God appear even there? If we pray that the will of God be done on earth as it is in heaven, are we not praying unaware that evil spirits remain on earth, where they have descended from heaven? There

are many on earth who become evil, because they are dominated by the cosmic powers above. If, however, we understand heaven in an allegorical sense, we maintain that it stands for Christ. In the same way, the earth symbolizes the Church. (Who is worthy to be the Father's throne, except Christ? What else can be a footstool for the feet of God, but the Church?) So, our difficulties are resolved. We say that every member of the Church is to pray to do the Father's will, as Christ did. He it was who came to do the will of the Father and he fulfilled that will perfectly. If we are united to him, we become one spirit with him. In this way, we do the will of God: it is fulfilled on earth, as it is in heaven.

5. It is not because of the place where a person lives, but because of an individual's disposition that one who is still on earth can be said to have *citizenship in heaven* and to *lay up treasures in heaven*. If one has his heart in heaven and *bears the image of the Man of Heaven*, that one no longer belongs to this earth nor to the lower world. He belongs to heaven and to the heavenly world that far surpasses this world. In the same way, *the spirits of wickedness* who still abide *in the heavenly realms* hold their *citizenship* on this earth. They connive to lay snares for us and to entrap us in battle. They lay up treasures on earth; they bear *the image* of the *inhabitants of this world, the first of God's handiwork, derided by the angels*. They do not belong to heaven, nor is their home there. They are too evil for that. Therefore, when we pray, *Thy will be done on earth as it is in heaven*, we ought not even think of these evil spirits. We ought, rather, remember that they, through pride, have descended with him who *fell like lightning from heaven*.

6. Perhaps, when our Savior tells us to pray that the Father's will be done on earth as it is in heaven, he is not giving us an absolute command to pray that those who are on earth in their bodies become like those who dwell in heaven. Rather, in urging us to pray in this manner, he wills that all living beings on the earth, even the lower species, grow to be like those superior to them who hold *citizenship in heaven*. Whoever is a sinner, no matter where he is, is earth. If he fails to repent, he will, indeed, become that

which he already resembles. But one who does the will of God, refusing to disobey his redeeming, spiritual laws, is already heaven.

If, then, we are still earth because of our sins, let us pray that God's will embrace and chastise us, in the same way that has been accomplished for those who have become heaven before us. If, in the eyes of God, we are not earth, but even now, heaven, let us pray that the will of God may be done on earth, among those lower beings, as that will is done in heaven. Thus, may the earth be made into heaven, as it were. Thus, one day, there will no longer be any earth, but all will have been transformed into heaven.

Chapter 29. 1. *And lead us not into temptation. But deliver us from evil.* Luke does not include the words, "But deliver us from evil." Since the Savior does not tell us to ask the impossible, I think we ought to examine why we are commanded to pray that we not enter "into temptation," despite the fact that our entire life on earth is a "temptation." On earth, we are surrounded on every side by the flesh. It "wars against the spirit"; its "thought is enmity of God." It cannot in any way be made "subject to the law of God." Because of this, we abide in a state of temptation.

5. One who does not examine closely the intention of the Lord in the command he gives might think that what he has taught us concerning prayer is contradicted by the words of the twenty-fifth Psalm: "Prove me, O Lord, and try me; burn my reins and my heart." Has anyone ever imagined that we are beyond the temptations of which we have been aware from the time we arrived at the ability to reason? Is there a time when any one of us can be sure that we do not have to struggle against sinning? Are we poor? Let us tremble, lest we "should" ever "steal and forswear" the "name of God." Are we rich? Let us not feel too secure. We may grow "full of lies" and, in our pride, think, "Who can see me?" Even Paul, though "rich in all utterance and in all knowledge," was not on that account freed from the danger of sinning through exalting himself. He needed "a sting of Satan to buffet him, lest he be exalted." If any one of us, conscious of our perfections, rises above all evil, let that one

read about Ezechias who, we are told in the Second Book of Paralipomenon fell because "his heart was lifted up."

9. Thus, we have seen, the whole "life of man on earth" is "temptation." Because of this, we ought to pray to be delivered from temptation. We do not pray that we not be tempted, for that is impossible for those who are still "on earth." We pray, rather, that we not yield to temptation. One who yields to temptation, I believe, enters into temptation because he becomes ensnared in its nets. Our Savior goes into these nets for the sake of those who had been caught in them previously. He looks "through the nets," as we read in the Canticle of Canticles, and speaks to those who, having been caught in them, have entered into temptation. He speaks to them as to a bride, saying, "Arise, come, my friend, my beautiful one, my dove."

Because I would point out that any time is a time of temptation for us, I add the following thought. Not even one who "meditates day and night on the law of God," seeking to put into practice the words, "the mouth of the just shall bring forth wisdom," — not even that person is free from temptation.

Chapter 30. When Luke writes, "Lead us not into temptation," it seems to me that he implies also, "Deliver us from evil." It is not at all unlikely that the Lord spoke in a more succinct manner to the disciple already advanced in knowledge, but in greater detail to the multitude who needed fuller instruction. Now, God "delivers us from evil," not when the Adversary refrains from attacking us with whatever tricks he has, but rather when we courageously face whatever comes to us and, thus, conquer him. This is the interpretation we give to the words, "Many are the afflictions of the just, but out of them all God delivers them." God delivers us from afflictions, not when afflictions no longer weigh upon us — for Paul says that we are at no time without affliction: "In all things we are afflicted." Rather, we are delivered when, though afflicted, with God's help, "we are not distressed." According to a Hebrew idiom, to be "afflicted" means to endure a critical situation that arises against a person's will. To be "distressed," on the contrary, refers to a state which does arise from the will to the extent that an individual is overcome by affliction and yields to it. Thus, Paul is right in saying, "In all things we are afflicted, but are not distressed." The same idea appears in the Psalms: "When I was in affliction, you granted me enlargement." Through the presence and assistance of the Word of God which encourages and saves us, our mind is enabled by God to be joyful and courageous in time of trial. This is the experience known as "enlargement."

3. Cyprian of Carthage

In the year A.D. 252, Cyprian, bishop of Carthage, composed a treatise on the Lord's Prayer. In this document, as in others written by Cyprian, we note a striking similarity to the earlier work of Tertullian. Indeed, this bishop daily instructed his secretary to bring him one of the "master's" works, that he might be instructed and edified. Cyprian, however, was more than an imitator of Tertullian, from whose teachings he departed on several points. His commentary on the Lord's Prayer is longer than that of the earlier African theologian's. Cyprian also introduced into his treatise a catechetical note, with an explanation of the rites of baptism. In contrast to the text of Origen, we find in Cyprian's work a more direct style and recognize the absence of the Alexandrian's allegorical reading of the Scriptural text.

Chapter 8.[27] Above all else, He who is the Teacher of peace and the Master of unity did not wish us to pray individually and privately as one would pray for oneself alone. We do not say, "My Father, who art in heaven." We do not pray, "Give me this day my bread." Neither does each one ask that his debt alone be forgiven, nor that she not be led into temptation. No one asks to be delivered from evil for oneself only. Our prayer is public and offered in common. When we pray, it is not for one person, but for the entire people; because, we

[27]Text: in CSEL 3, ed. Von Hartel 3. Von Hartel.

the whole people, are one. God, who is the Teacher of prayer
and peace, taught us peace. He wished each one to pray for
all, just as he, himself, has borne all together in one. The three
children in the fiery furnace observed this law. They were
united as one in their prayer; they were in harmony with one
another in the Spirit. The divine Scriptures affirm in faith
how they prayed, giving us an example to imitate in our
prayers, so that we might become like them. "Then those
three, as if from one mouth, sang a hymn and blessed God."
They spoke as if with one mouth, although Christ had not
yet taught them to pray. The words they offered in prayer
were fruitful and efficacious, because prayer that is full of
peace, simple and spiritual, appeals to the Lord. The Apostles and disciples also prayed in this manner, after the Lord's
Ascension: "They all with one mind persevered in prayer
with the woman and Mary, the mother of Jesus, and with his
brethren." With a united mind, they persevered in prayer. By
their steadfastness and their unity in prayer, they proclaimed that God, who makes those who are of one mind to
dwell together in one house, admits to the eternal, divine
home, only those who are found to be of one mind in prayer.

Chapter 14.   We also say: 'Thy will be done in heaven as
it is on earth.' We do not pray in order that God may do
what he will, but that we may be able to do his will. Who,
indeed, can prevent God from doing what he wills? The
devil, however, prevents our mind and our actions from
obeying God in everything. Thus, we pray and ask earnestly
that the will of God be accomplished in us. If God's will is to
be done in us, we have need of God's will. That is, we need
his protection and his assistance. Not one of us is strong
enough in his own strength. We have assurance of safety,
however, in the generosity and the mercy of God.

The Lord, too, manifested the weakness of the humanity
which he had assumed when he prayed, at the end, "Father,
if it be possible, let this cup pass from me." Then, in order
that his disciples might learn to do God's will rather than
their own, he gave them an example in these words, "Yet,
not my will, but thine be done."

In another place, we read that the Lord said, "I have come down from heaven, not to do my own will, but the will of him who sent me." Now, if the Son became obedient in order to do his Father's will, should not the servant, even more, obey, in order to accomplish his Lord's will? In his epistle, John urges us to do the will of God. he instructs us by saying, "Do not set your hearts on the godless world or anything in it. Anyone who loves the world is a stranger to the Father's love. Everything the world affords, all that panders to the appetites or entices the eyes, all the glamour of its life, springs not from the Father but from the godless world. And that world is passing away with all its allurements, but he who does God's will stands for evermore." We who desire to stand forevermore ought to do the will of the eternal God.

Chapter 25. It is necessary, too, that the Lord admonish us to pray in this way, "And lead us not into temptation." In this petition, we learn that the adversary has no power against us, unless God has already permitted it. This is shown so that all our reverence, devotion and obedience may be given to God. In temptation, nothing evil is permitted against us, unless God allows it.

Chapter 26. Indeed, power is granted against us in two ways. Either it is given for punishment when we sin, or for glory when we are blessed. We see this in the case of Job, when God spoke these words: "Behold, all that he possesses is in your hands; only do not touch his person." In the gospel, at the time of the Lord's passion, he says, "You would have no power at all over me, unless it were given you from on high." Morever, when we pray that we not enter into temptation, we are made to recall our weakness and our limitations, lest one in insolence extol himself; another, in pride and arrogance, claim something for himself; a third claim as his own the glory of a martyr's witness or suffering. The Lord has taught us humility, in saying, "Watch and pray that you may not enter into temptation. The spirit, indeed, is willing, but the flesh is weak." When we begin with humble, submissive confession and attribute all glory to God, whatever we pray for in reverence and gratitude may be granted by his loving kindness.

Chapter 27. After these things have been said, the prayer is summed up in a little phrase that brings our petitions and intercession to an end, quickly and in a few words. At the very end, we pray, "But deliver us from evil." By this, we include all the trials which the enemy seeks to inflict on us in this world. We can find strong and faithful protection against such evil, if God delivers us and if he grants us his aid, as we pray and beseech him. When we say, "Deliver us from evil," there is nothing left to ask for. Once we have sought and obtained God's protection against evil, we are safe and secure against all the works of the devil and the evils of the world. Who of us can be afraid of the world, if God is for us as our protector?

4. *Gregory of Nyssa*

Gregory of Nyssa (c. A.D. 335 — c. A.D. 394) is more popularly known as one of the Cappadocian Fathers. As the younger brother of the great Basil of Caesarea and the "second" Gregory in this triumvirate, he has frequently been overshadowed and, still today, relatively few of his works are available in English translation. Those who do know Gregory of Nyssa, however, respect him as a theologian whose contributions place him among the greatest writers of the patristic age. He is also recognized for his spiritual, mystical doctrine, in which the influence of his "master," Origen can be found.

Gregory's treatise on the Lord's Prayer is composed of five sermons in which he develops one of his favorite themes, addresses the evils of his day and seeks, as a good pastor, to provide the spiritual care needed by his people. Gregory seems never to have tired of proclaiming that our souls are made in the Divine Image; tarnished by sin, we are to be restored to the original beauty of the *imago Dei* within us. This means learning to pray in the right way and for the right things. The Lord's Prayer is the model for our right praying.

Gregory used practical examples to bring his lessons home to the people. He frequently drew on the scientific data of his day. We can see this in Sermon 4 (*Thy Will be done, on earth as it is in Heaven. Give us this day our daily bread.*), which begins with an exposition on the subject of bodily health and the advice of a "medical expert" for curing disease through a restoration of "natural balance." Gregory's reflections on the third petition of the Lord's prayer are developed against the background of the medical theory to which he has referred.[28]

Sermon 2. *When you pray, say: Our Father, who art in Heaven.* In one of the Psalms the great David asks, "Who will give me wings like a dove?" I, too, would boldly use the same words. Who is there to give me those wings by which my mind might take its flight to the heights envisioned in the noble words of this petition? Leaving behind all that is of earth, I would advance and move through the middle air. I would attain to the beauty of ethereal space, reach the stars and contemplate their order and arrangement. However, I would not stop even there. Progressing beyond them, I would abandon as alien everything subject to movement and change. Then I would, at last, perceive that Nature which is immutable, the unchanging Power existing in its own right, as it guides and sustains all things in being — for all are dependent on the ineffable will of Divine Wisdom. Thus must my mind, detached from all that is subject to motion, flux and change, come to rest quietly in a spiritual repose without movement. Then will I be made like him who is perfectly unchangeable. Then will I be able to address him by that intimate name and say, "Father."

What spirit must there be in a person who would pronounce this word! What trust! What a pure conscience! Let us suppose that a man might seek to know God as much as possible, by considering the names that have been invented for the Deity and thus arrive at an understanding of God's

[28]Adapted from translation by Hilda C. Graef ACW 18. Westminster, Maryland: The Newman Press, 1954) Text: PG44, 1119-1194).

ineffable glory. That man would learn that, whatever the Divine Nature is in itself, it is absolute goodness, holiness, joy, power, glory and purity. It is eternity, absolutely and always the same. Considering these things and all things besides that thought could learn through the Sacred Scriptures or through meditation, could anyone dare to utter this word and call God Father? If a man has any sense, he would, surely, not dare to call God by this name, Father, since he does not find in himself the things he sees in God.

Therefore, if the Lord in his prayer teaches us to call God Father, it would seem that what he is doing is giving us as our law the most sublime law. Truth does not teach us to deceive by saying we are something we are not or by using a name to which we have no claim. . . . Therefore, it is dangerous for us to dare to offer this prayer and to call God our Father before our lives have been purified.

Sermon 4. At one time, we humans, as intelligent beings, were healthy, for the movements of our soul, which correspond to the elements of the universe, were balanced evenly within us, in every manner in the harmony of virtue. Then, the element of concupiscence became dominant, defeating its opposite, continence, as a strong enemy overpowers a conquered warrior. No longer were the inordinate desires for things forbidden held in check. In this way, the fatal disease of sin was introduced into our human nature. For this reason, the true Physician of the diseases of our soul shared our life so as to heal those who were ill. He gradually lessens the root of the disease through the meaning of this prayer. Thus are we restored by him to spiritual health.

Now the health of our soul is the fulfillment of the divine Will, even as the disease that leads to death for the soul is failure to do the good that is this Will. We fell into sickness when we abandoned the healthful way of life in Paradise, to fill ourselves with disobedience, a poison that overcame our nature through an evil, deadly disease. The true Physician then came to follow the law of medicine, healing us fully through introducing into our being a healing contrary to the sickness. He frees from illness those who had fallen prey to disease by separation from God's Will and does this by uniting them again to this divine Will. It is the words of this prayer which bring about the cure of the soul's disease. Our Physician prays as if his own soul were steeped in pain: *Thy Will be done.* For the Will of God is our salvation. If, then, we are to say: Thy Will be done in me, also, it is absolutely necessary that we, first of all, renounce all that is opposed to this Will, confessing humbly all the evil we have done.

What we mean to say is this: the will that has been opposed to God throughout my life has brought evil to my soul. I have served a wicked master and have become the executioner of my own soul. Have mercy on me! Relieve my misery! Grant that now, at last, thy Will may be fulfilled in me. Just as darkness is dispelled when light penetrates a cave, so too, when thy Will is done in me, every evil, wicked tendency of my free will is reduced to nothing. Then, continence will overcome the unbridled impulses of passion that dominate my mind. Humility will conquer haughtiness and modesty will heal the ravages of pride. Charity, that highest good, will cast out of my soul a multitude of contrary evils. In the presence of charity, hate, envy, anger and all the violent reactions of our emotions disappear. With charity in our hearts, there is no room for us to be hypocritical or traiterous; there is no place to nurse injuries or plot revenge. Charity brings peace to the agitated heart and the covetous eye. When charity rules our lives, every evil is effaced. Thus does the Will of God overcome and triumph over the two-fold idolatry of slavery to false gods and of covetousness for gold and silver, which the prophet calls the idols of the Gentiles. For this do we pray, Thy Will be done, so that the will of the Evil One may be destroyed.

What does the next phrase mean: *on earth as it is in heaven*? It seems to me that, perhaps, these words signify a deeper teaching, concerning knowledge of the Divine Mind through contemplation of a creature.

In other words, all of rational creation is divided into

corporeal and incorporeal natures. Angels are incorporeal; we are bodily. Spiritual beings, separated from the weight of the earthly body — solid and heavy, dwell in the higher region, in light and in the ethereal places. They are nimble and agile. Our nature, however, of necessity is assigned to an earthly life because our body which is derived from the dust of the earth, is related to what is earthly. I do not know why the divine Will ordained this to be so. Perhaps it was done that the whole creation might achieve a harmony with itself: the lower region having a share in what is of heaven, and heaven itself sharing in those things that are of the earth. Thus would the creation of man bring to each realm a participation in what belongs to the other. For the spiritual soul is clearly in harmony with spiritual and heavenly beings, though it dwells in an earthly body. In the final restoration, our earthly flesh will be taken up with the soul into the heavenly places.

Since, then, life in the upper regions is pure and free from enslavement to the turmoil of the passions, while here below we are caught in every kind of misery and distress, we should understand clearly that the heavenly city, from which all evil is absent, is firmly founded in the goodness of the Will of God. Where there is no evil, there is, of necessity, good. Our life, however, which has fallen away from things that are good, has also fallen away from the divine Will. Hence, this prayer teaches us that our lives must be purified from evil, so that the Will of God may reign in us, as it does in heaven, without obstacle or delay. It is as if we prayed: Just as thy Will is fulfilled by Thrones and Principalities, by Powers and Dominations and all the hosts above the earth in that realm where good is never restrained or prevented by evil, so may what is good be accomplished in us also. Then, when all that is evil has been removed from us, thy Will shall be fulfilled in all ways in our souls.

Sermon 5. (This sermon is a commentary on several petitions: "Forgive us our debts, as we forgive our debtors. And lead us not into temptation. But deliver us from evil.")

What is the meaning of the phrase that follows immediately after *as we forgive our debtors*? This is something that ought not to be passed over without consideration. We ought to know what we are praying for. We ought to offer the petition with our soul, not only with our lips: *Lead us not into temptation, but deliver us from evil.* My friends, what do these words mean? It seems that the Lord gives many different names to the evil one, each suited to the difference among evil actions. So, he is devil, Beelzebub, Mammon, prince of this world, murderer of humankind, the evil one, the father of lies, and other similar names. Perhaps, in this instance, one of the names attributed to him is "temptation." The juxtaposition of the words confirms this thought. After we say, "Lead us not into temptation," the Lord says that we should be delivered from evil, as if both words meant the same thing. If a man who does not enter into temptation is removed far from evil; if one who has entered into temptation is, of necessity, involved with evil, then the two words, temptation and the evil one, refer to the same thing. Then, what does this petition teach us? The Lord exhorts us to be separated from the things of this world, as when he taught his disciples, "the entire world is seated in wickedness." Therefore, if a person desires to be free from that which is wicked, that one will find it necessary to be separated from the world. Temptation has no opportunity to touch a soul, unless preoccupation with the world and things of the world be thrown out to the greedy on the hook of evil, like bait.... Let us rise up and pray to God, "Lead us not into temptation" — into the evils of the world — "but deliver us from evil," which reigns in the world. May we be delivered from this through Christ's grace. His is the power and the glory, with the Father and the Holy Spirit, now and ever and forever and ever. Amen.

5. Cyril of Jerusalem

Cyril, bishop of Jerusalem in the fourth century, is best known to us as the author of a series of catechetical lectures which have been described by Quasten as "one of the most precious treasures of Christian antiquity"

(*Patrology*, III). The twenty-four lectures consist of an introductory *Protocatechesis*, eighteen pre-baptismal instructions and five Mystagogic (post-baptismal) lectures. In the fifth of the instructions given to the newly baptized, Cyril presents his explanation of the Lord's Prayer. In sections eight to ten, Cyril presents the meaning and importance of the intercessions offered during the celebration of the Eucharist. In section eleven, he begins his commentary, giving us the first witness to the inclusion of the *Pater* in the eucharistic liturgy. His text is brief in striking contrast to the selections above. In it, we can find an echo and a distillation of themes found in earlier writers.

5 (23) 11.[29] Then, after that, you recite this prayer which the Savior entrusted to his own disciples. With a pure conscience, you address God by the name, Father, and you say, "Our Father, who art in heaven." How great is the gracious kindness of God! He grants such pardon and so generous a share in grace to those who have abandoned him and have fallen into the worst of evils that they are able to call him Father: Our Father who art in heaven. Here, "heaven" can well be understood as those who bear the image of the celestial world in themselves, in whom God abides and with whom he walks.

5 (23), 14. *Thy will be done on earth as it is in heaven.* The angels of God, divine and blessed spirits, do the Will of God. David tells us this when he sings, "Bless the Lord, all you his angels, you who are mighty in strength, doing the things he wills." When you pray in these words, then, you are, in fact, saying, "As your Will is fulfilled in the angels, Lord, let it be done also on earth in me."

5 (23) 17. "And lead us not into temptation," Lord. Does the Lord teach us to ask that we never be tempted? Why, then, is it written elsewhere, "The man who is not tempted has not been proven"; and again, "My friends, count it as perfect joy when you fall into many temptations"? But,

[29]Text SC 126 adaptations.

perhaps to enter into temptation means to be overcome by temptation. Indeed, temptation is like a torrent of water that is difficult to cross. Thus, some persons are not drowned in temptations. They cross the torrent as if they were excellent swimmers, without being carried away by it. Others, without the same qualities, once they have entered the rushing stream, are overcome. Thus, for example, Judas entered into the temptation to avarice. He could not begin to swim, but, overcome as it were both corporally and spiritually, was suffocated in its waves. Peter entered into the temptation to denial, but once caught there, he was able to swim energetically, was not overcome and was saved.

Listen also, again, to the chorus of unconquered saints who sing praise and thanks for having been saved from temptations: "You have put us to the test, O God. You have led us through fire, like silver refined in the furnace. You have caused us to be caught in a snare; you have heaped tribulations upon our back; you have let men stand over our heads. We have passed through fire and water and you have led us to a place of refreshment." Do you see them speaking with confidence of their crossing without having been drowned in its depths? "You have led us to a place of refreshment." Entry into a place of refreshment is the same thing as being saved from temptation.

18. "But deliver us from the Evil One." If the words, "Lead us not into temptation" meant not to be tempted in any way at all, (the Lord) would not add, "But deliver us from the Evil One." The Evil One is our adversary, the devil, from whom we ask to be delivered.

Chapter Seven

Poets and Musicians Pray

Through the petitions of the Lord's prayer, Christians developed a catholic mind and heart: they learned to think and feel in a universal dimension, interceding with the Father in and through Jesus Christ, for all in need. This universal dimension found other expressions, as well. Irenaeus taught that all human beings, with their history and their experience, were being "recapitulated"—completed, fulfilled, purified, perfected—in and through Christ and his saving work. Clement of Alexandria and Origen boasted that nothing of interest to the human intellect was foreign to their *Didascalia*, the catechetical-theological school of Alexandria.

It is not to be wondered at, then, that Christian doctrine and theology were to find their way into art, music and poetry. Here, we are interested, particularly, in the literary forms that reflected at a level accessible to large numbers of people the issues and questions debated at another level by the great theological leaders of the day. We are also interested in the way in which Christians prayed in song and verse and rhyme.

1. Clement of Alexandria.

The publication, in 1962, of an Essay on Clement of Alexandria by Thomas Merton, along with the Trappist monk's translation of selections from Clement's *The Pro-*

treptikos (New York: New Directions), highlighted the poetic achievement of "one of the first and most appealing of the Ancient Christian Writers." Clement, a second century Greek convert to Christianity, is known as the Father of Christian Humanism and the first Christian scholar. He preceded Origen as director of the *Didascalia*. The following selection is taken from the conclusion of Clement's work, *Christ the Educator (Paidagogos)*. It is one of the earliest Christian hymns recorded in Greek.

HYMN TO THE EDUCATOR[30]

Bridle, mastering unbroken foals,
Wing of the never-wearied bird,
Steady rudder of ships at sea,
Shepherd of the King's own flock:
Call your children together,
Bid them, in their innocence, sing
A song of holy praise,
Hymns from the heart;
Let them chant melodies from pure lips
To Christ, their leader and their guide.
You reign over the saints,
Conqueror of the world,
Word and Son of the Most High God, the heavenly Father,
Citadel of Wisdom,
Sure comforter of all who suffer,
Eternal Joy of the ages,
Jesus, you are the Savior
Of our mortal race.
Shepherd and laborer,
Rudder and bridle,
Wing, bearing aloft to the heavens a sanctified flock;
Fisher of those men and women
Who have not been swallowed up in an ocean of wickedness,

---

[30]Greek text: Staehlin, second edition; *GCS Schriftsteller der Ersten Drei Jahrhunderte*, 1956. SC 158.

Unsullied fish drawn by the sweet bait of life out of the
violent tempest.
O Holy Shepherd of the lambs of the Word,
Be their guide. O King of innocent children,
Christ, they wind their way toward heaven,
Walking in your footsteps.

O Word, eternal well-spring,
Time without end,
Eternal Light,
Fountain of true piety,
You are the artisan of virtue in those whose holy lives are a
hymn to God.
Christ Jesus, drawn from the tender breasts of your bride as
gifts
From your wisdom,

    You are the celestial milk,
    Held in the tender breasts of your bride,
    As a gift of your wisdom, distilled through the burden of
suffering.

Your little children, with innocent lips,
Drink the nectar of the Spirit
From the bosom of the Word, their Mother
Until they are fully satisfied.

    Let us celebrate the royalty of Christ,
    Praising him without affection, in all simplicity.
    Let us offer him a holy tribute,
    Singing in unity the lessons we have learned from his Life.
    Let us join in the procession of those
    Who follow the Omnipotent Son.

Choir of those who love peace,
Heirs of Christ,
Wisdom-people:
Let us, together, glorify
The God of peace!

2. *Marius Victorinus*

Marius Victorinus is best known, in many circles, as the aged pagan, Neoplatonic philosopher whose conversion to Christianity so deeply touched the great Augustine (*Confessions*, Book VIII, chapters 2, 4, 5): "I burned to imitate him." His importance as a Christian writer seems to rest on his position "at the crossroads of three different paths: the traditions of classical Rome — Cicero Virgil; the new trends in philosophic thought — Plotinus, *Porphyry*; the new positions of Christianity, with the crisis in conscience these brought for the Roman citizen."[31]

Victorinus is the first of the Christian Latin workers to undertake a systematic treatise on the Trinity. His influence on St. Augustine's later work, *De trinitate*, cannot be denied.

The following selection is taken from the poetry, rather than from the prose works of Victorinus. It is one of the earliest examples of the way in which theology and doctrine were expressed in writings other than treatises.

SECOND HYMN[32]

Have mercy on me, Lord! O Christ, have mercy on me!
Have mercy on me, Lord,
For I have believed in you,
Have mercy on me, Lord,
Because of your mercy, I have come to know you!

Have mercy on me, Lord! Christ, have mercy on me!
You are the *Logos* of my mind!
You are the *Logos* of my soul!
You are the *Logos* of my body!

Have mercy on me, Lord! Christ, have mercy on me!
God lives,

---

[31] *Marius Victorinus*, Mary T. Clark, R.S.C.J., trans. The FOTC 69.5: The Catholic University of America Press, 1981; p.5.

[32] PL VIII; SC 68

God lives eternally and
Because nothing is before He is, God lives of His own Being.

Have mercy on me, Lord! Christ, have mercy on me!
Christ lives, and
Because, in begetting him, God granted that he live of
himself,
Because he does live of himself, Christ lives eternally.

Have mercy on me, Lord! Christ, have mercy on me!
Because God lives, because he lives eternally,
Eternal life has been begotten;
This eternal life is Christ, the Son of God.

Have mercy on me, Lord! Christ, have mercy on me!
Now, if the Father lives of his own Being,
If the Son also lives of his own being,
Thanks to the Father's generation,
He is of one Being with the Father since he, also, lives
eternally.

Have mercy on me, Lord! Christ, have mercy on me!
O God, you have given me a soul.
But the soul is the image of life, since the soul, too, lives.
O God, grant that my soul may also live eternally!

Have mercy on me, Lord! Christ, have mercy on me!
If I have been created in your likeness, Father God,
And in the image of your Son,
Grant that I may live, created for the ages,
For the Son has known me.

Have mercy on me, Lord! Christ, have mercy on me!
I have loved the world, for you have made it;
I have been a prisoner of the world, when it has become
jealous
Of all that belongs to you.
Now, I hate the world, for I have drunk of the Spirit.

Have mercy on me, Lord! Christ, have mercy on me!
Lord, help those who have fallen!
Help those who seek to rise again!

Because of your divine decree and your holy judgment,
Even my sin has its share in the mystery of salvation!

May I, at last, rest in the dwelling-place of light,
Saved by your grace!

3. *Ephrem, Harp of the Holy Spirit*

St. Ephrem is one of the most radiant witnesses of early
Christian Syria. As a deacon, he fulfilled the offices of
that ministry for nearly fifty years, assistant to his
bishops as preacher and homilist, catechist and director
of liturgy, leader of prayer and sacred music, dispenser of
goods to the poor, servant of the sick and the stranger,
model of the ascetical life as of the life of contemplation.
Ephrem's hymns became effective instruments in the
struggle against heresy. They have been translated into
Greek, Armenian, Georgian, Ethiopian, Latin and
Slavonic.

The two hymns presented below are taken from the
collection, "On Paradise." They are rich in biblical image-
ry and full of enthusiasm for that Promised Land to
which we are called, with the assurance of entry through
the grace of Christ who has preceded us, yet accompanies
us on our pilgrimage.[33]

HYMN V

Refrain: Happy are they who deserve to inherit your Paradise!

1. Then shall I contemplate the Creator-Word
      And I shall compare Him
   To the Rock which accompanied the people
      Through the desert.
   Without collecting or accumulating
      Water for itself,

[33]This is the description given in René Lavenant, S.J., *Ephrem de Nisibe:
Hymnes Sur le Paradis, SC 137.8*

It poured forth upon the people
    Abundant torrents.
No water was within this Rock,
    Yet oceans of water flowed from it.
So, too, the Word created its works
    Out of nothing.
2. In his Book,
    Moses describes the creation of all of Nature,
So that witness might be given to the Creator
    By both Nature and the Book.
Nature witnesses as it is used;
    The Book, when it is read.
These are the witnesses
    Which are diffused everywhere,
Which appear in every age,
    Which are present to each new moment;
They prove to those who are unfaithful
    How ungrateful they are to their Creator.
3. I began to read the beginning of this Book
    And I trembled with joy:
Its verses, its every line
    Opened arms wide to take me in.
The first verse came running gladly toward me,
    Embracing me and leading me forward
    to meet its companion.
When I reached the line
    Where the story of Paradise is written,
It carried me from the heart of the Book
    Into the very heart of the Garden.
4. The lines were like a bridge
    For my eyes and my spirit
To cross together,
    To enter together the story of Eden.
As my eyes read,
    They transported my spirit across the bridge;
My spirit, in turn, knew how to bring rest
    To my eyes, in their reading.
For, as the Book was being read,
    As my eyes rested, my spirit labored.

5. As I discovered both the bridge and the door to Paradise
       Within this Book,
     I passed over and entered.

   As for my eyes, they remained outside,
       But my spirit entered the heart of the Garden.
   I went everywhere in that place,
       Though it is not described:
   Radiantly clear is that mountain-top,
       Undefiled, sublime, splendid!
   In the Book, it is called Eden:
       The place of all pleasure.
6. There, too, I beheld the tents
           Of the Just,
   Filled with perfume,
       Fragrant with aromas,
   Garlanded with fruits,
       Crowned with flowers.
   As a man labored,
       So did his dwelling appear:
   One was scarcely adorned,
       Another dazzled with splendor:
   One was tarnished and dull in color,
       Another shone with glory.
7. Then, again, I asked myself this question:
       Is Paradise enough to satisfy
   The Just who must abide there?
   I looked for an "unwritten" answer
   And found enlightenment in what was "written":
   "Consider that man
       In whom a Legion of devils dwell;
   Without anyone's even imagining it,
       They took up residence in him,
   For their army is even more subtle
       Than the soul!"
8. Now this entire legion
       Abode within one single body.
   But the bodies of the Just will be

One hundred times more ethereal,
And one hundred times more subtle,
   When they are raised up at the resurrection.
That body will appear in the image
   Of a royal spirit:
As it wills, it will expand and extend itself;
As it chooses, it will withdraw and diminish in size.
When it draws back, it is here;
When it spreads out, it is everywhere.

9. There is more. Listen and understand:
   Lamps that shine out through a thousand rays
   Enlighten a single house;
The calyx of a single flower
   Holds thousands of perfumes.
Even though they may be contained in the smallest of
   spaces,
They spread abroad in the air
   As if to celebrate a feast:
So too, Paradise,
   Although it is filled with spirits,
Has room to spare for their celebrations.

10. I can say even more than this:
   An infinite number of thoughts
   Dwell in the smallest heart
And, while there, are everywhere more than anywhere
else.
They are not constrained,
   Neither are they a burden to that heart.
How much more, then, will Paradise
   Provide enough space for those spiritual beings
Whose pure substance cannot be touched,
   Even by a thought!
Let us give praise for this wonder!

11. I marveled to the full extent of my being;
   When I returned to myself,
I suddenly heard from the depths of Paradise
   A mighty thunder
And the blare of trumpets,

As in a camp.
There was the sound, also, of voices crying out:
"All Hail to the Thrice-Holy!"
It was, then, in the midst of Paradise
That Divinity dwelt—
Praised be Our God!
I should have known it would be so,
Since the place was empty.
The voices confirmed my thought with certainty.

12. Once again, Eden filled me with rapture,
Because of its peace, because of its beauty.
There, one finds
An untarnished beauty;
There is ever
An inalterable peace.
Happy are they
Who deserve to have this bestowed on them—
If not out of justice,
At least, through goodness;
If not because of their works,
At least, through compassion and mercy.

13. In crossing the border into Paradise,
I had been astonished
To find contained and restrained therein
Everything that assures good health.
When I returned to the shores of the earth,
Mother of thorns,
Sorrows and evils of every kind
Rushed upon me.
I learned, then, that this land of ours,
In comparison with that other,
Is a prison for which captives weep,
When they are about to leave it.

14. I was amazed to see that children,
Scarcely out of the womb, also weep.
They cry as they leave darkness for light,
Confinement for an entire universe.
So is death a sort of birth for human beings.
Those who are born weep as they leave this world,

The Mother of sorrows,
Even as they go forth to enter a Garden of Delights.
15. Lord of Paradise,
Have mercy on me!
If I am not able to enter your Paradise,
At least, grant that I be worthy
To remain close to its boundaries.
Within, a table is set for the holy ones!
Let the fruits of this garden
Fall in torrents of crumbs
For us sinners
Who will live, there, because of your Goodness!

HYMN XIV

Refrain: Grant us the grace
To welcome your Kingdom
With hosannas of praise!
1. We all have to submit to daily suffering,
In the smallest things.
It is an experience that is meant to wean us
From this earthly life
And yet, despite what we learn,
Our spirit clings to this world!
Happy are they who have understood
How useful it is
To provide supplies for the journey—
Good works — to welcome
The Lord we encounter!
Happy are they whose earnings
Will rejoice the heart of their Master!
2. Alas! We are like a slave who refuses
The freedom offered him
In the seventh year of his labors!
He prefers that his ear be pierced,
That he may remain for life
A slave of those who are also slaves!
See, thanks to death,
The persecuted, the pure of heart,
All those whom you led to the tomb for burial,

Obtain deliverance.
Pray that you may deserve to greet your friends!
3. Jeremiah was thrown
    Into the pit of Jonathan's house.
    Although he was a patient man,
        He did not desire to stay there.
    But we, whose earthly dwelling
        Is packed with malice,
    We pray that we be left in it,
    Never seeing that we are drowning there!
    Grant, Lord, that we may see clearly
        The state of that place which holds us prisoners!
4. We learn that Daniel prayed
        To be released from Babylon
    In order to go to the Promised Land.
    Babylon is an image of the earth accursed.
    For our benefit, the Lord ordained this image,
    That we might pray to enter the land of Eden.
    Blessed is He whose goodness leads us to our goal!
5. Noah, too, waited and prayed, symbolically,
        For freedom to leave the Ark,
    When staying in it was no inconvenience for him!
    Oh, that we might no longer be attached
        To this earthy dwelling,
    This port of every ill!
    Happy are they who steer their ship
        Straight toward Paradise!
6. Moses was held in high honor in Egypt.
    But, he would not let himself be known
        As "the son of Pharoah's daughter."
    He preferred to live as a poor man, a shepherd.
    What, then, should be our joy,
        When we go forth
    From slavery to liberty!
    Happy are they who find deliverance
        In Paradise!
7. Jacob led his flock straight to his father's house:
    Here is a symbol for those who can discern,
        A parable for those who understand:

This is the way for us to go to the father's house.
Let us, too, my brothers and sisters,
    Return to the house of our Father,
Without being seduced by love
    Of a world that is passing away.
Let Eden be your true city!
Happy are they who will see their beloved friends again,
in Eden!

8. There, we find the fruits of holiness,
        Apparel of light,
    Crowns of victory,
        Steps to the highest abodes,
    Wealth that does not sate us,
        Relief without distress,
    An endless feast for all eternity!
    But, in this place of torment,
    Happy are those of us who say,
        "Lord, deliver me!"

9. The language of that heavenly abode
        Is the singing of blessed spirits,
    As Seraphim chant
        And Cherubim wings rustle!
    There is nothing on earth to equal such sounds!
    Their only delight is to give forth praise.
    Each one nourishes his soul
        With the music of a harp.
    Come, Lord! make us worthy to sing with them
        A chorus of "Hosannas."

10. Let us now try to lift the veil a little
        From our eyes
    And contemplate this place, this Eden.
    Let us try to stir up in our hearts
        A feeling of regret
    That we must prolong our stay
        In this port of storm-wrecked vessels,
    Where sea-merchants suffer daily losses
        With worm-eaten ships and plundered cargoes.
    Happy the children who have completed the voyage
        In safety!

11. They feed as lambs freed from all fear
      In the meadows of Paradise.
    Satan is miserable, because he could not
      Destroy their purity.
    Those who could not lead them astray
      Are seized by envy.
    Their virgin purity reigns,
      Radiant and royal,
    Crowning their unsullied, unblemished brows.
    Happy are they who will be worthy
      To join them!

12. Their beauty will never fade,
      Their splendor will never die.
    While their sense-bereft parents weep and mourn.
    There they praise the One whom they might never have known,
      Here on this earth.
    They praise the One whose gentleness is touched
      By our tears, our lamentations and our rent garments.
    Blessed be He at whom we direct our anger!
      He has exalted our beloved dead in glory.

13. Glory be to the Gardener of the Tree of Humanity,
      Who daily gathers for the offering
      Fruits of every size and age and condition!
    Behold this wonder: gentle flowers are picked
      Before ripened fruits!
    Blessed be He who offers a crown of infants
      To his heavenly Father!

14. There above, remorse will fill the hearts of many
      Who did not bear trial and chastisement.
    God who is Good would have them pay their debt
      Through minor, passing trials—but they would not!
    Rightly will they regret the Goodness they did not know.
    All will praise You, God! Because
      You are Infinite Goodness for everyone!

15. Oh! grant that Your Goodness may lead me, also,
      For I, too, am a prisoner!

My parents were led captive
From the Garden of Eden
Into this land of thorns, deceived by Satan.
He proved himself a liar, trying to trick me
    Into cherishing and loving this wicked earth,
    A dwelling-place of chastisement.
Blessed is He who comes to set prisoners free
    And to destroy the one who took us captive!

4. *Gregory of Nazianzus*

Gregory, sometimes known as the "Theologian," was one of the three great Fathers known as the Cappadocians. With his friend, Basil of Caesarea, and Basil's younger brother, Gregory of Nyssa, the Nazianzen brought theological, spiritual and pastoral leadership to the Church in the fourth century. In addition to the profound theological *Orations* for which he is known, Gregory's writings include letters and poems. The following text is an excerpt from a work unique of its kind in patristic literature: a tragic drama; specifically, a Euripidesian Cento. It was only in 1969, with the publication of the text in the edition of *Sources Chrétiennes* that a centuries-old debate regarding the authorship of this work seems to have been resolved in favor of Gregory of Nazianzus, "Théologian par excellence." The following excerpt (11. 2532-2602), a prayer to Christ and his mother, concludes the recital of the Passion and Death, Christ in the Tomb and the Resurrection.[34]

THE PASSION OF CHRIST

Omnipotent King, redeemer most excellent, my Savior,
    deliver me from these indissoluble bonds
In which, alas, I have been imprisoned because of
    my weakness;

[34]*La Passion du Christ*, Grégoire de Nazianz: ed. André Tuilier *SC 149.*

Our enemy, the Seducer, has pursued me in his jealousy,
Seeing that I had been delivered from my past faults
    through trust in you, by a gift of your great goodness.
Hail! Incomparable Son of an incomparable Father!
My King and Sovereign, you have crushed the serpent,
    the cause of all our ills.
You have conquered our most fearful enemy, death.
Do not abandon me again into the power of these foes.
King, eternal King, you are the omnipotent God
    and the infinitely just judge, come to judge me.
How do I dare look on you, O Word?
How will my eyes contemplate your majesty,
For, in my misery, I have proven myself unworthy
    of heaven, earth and all your creation?
The Evil One has seized me, has cast me into
    the chasm, the abyss, into immense chaos.
Relentlessly, he has pursued me until, having me
    in his grasp,
He has cast me totally into the darkness of hell.
Have mercy on me, my God; stretch out your hands
    to me; sustain me.
Do not abandon me to the whims of humankind's foe.
I am your creature: instruct me, divine Word;
    admonish me yourself here below, in your great goodness;
Do not permit me to be cast into hell.
We who have been guilty of
    miserable injustice in our bodies
Beg you, redeemer, to hear us:
We have sinned against you; we have often violated
    your commandments.
We have understood too late; we have not known what
    was necessary when we ought;
Moreover, we have not yet done what is pleasing
    in your sight.
We confess our faults; do you pardon them;
We know that your anger is not like that of mortal beings.
Have mercy on me, O Savior; do not let me die
    because of my faults.

I am your child, the child of your own handmaiden.
I am the one for whom you have died, divine Word.
Do not abandon me to the whims of the Evil One.
Instruct me according to your commandment; teach me
    in your great goodness.
Recognize, O Word of God, that those who intercede
    for us are your own Mother and your followers
To whom you have given the grace to free us from our
bonds.

O sovereign Virgin, noble and blessed Lady, you dwell in
    heaven, in the abode of the elect.
You have shaken off the burden of human existence to be
    clothed in the apparel of immortality.
We know that, like God, you are ever young.
In the heights of heaven, accept my prayers
    with kindness.
Yes, yes! most glorious Virgin, receive my prayers.
Among all mortal beings, you alone possess the privilege
    of being Mother of the Word, in a way beyond all
    understanding.
For this reason, I place my confidence in you;
It is my turn to present my prayers to you and so,
    I offer you, Lady,
A crown woven of flowers from a virgin meadow
    in exchange for the graces with which you have
    favored me.
Protect me always from every evil, from visible enemies
    and, yet more, from invisible foes.
May I cross the last threshold of my life as I have
    begun it—with you ever as my guardian;
Be, at all times, my all-powerful advocate with your Son,
    in the company of those holy ones so pleasing to him!
Do not allow me to be delivered up to torture for
    having been the plaything of the Evil One,
    the corrupter of souls.
Protect me; preserve me from flames of fire and
    from darkness.

Let the faith and grace that are yours be efficacious
    for my justification,
For it is well known that God's grace comes to us
    through your intercession.
And now, I want to sing a hymn of gratitude to you:
Hail, O Woman! You are all joy!
Virgin Mother, you are the most beautiful of all virgins.
Sovereign Mistress, it is you who command the hosts of
heaven.
O Lady, O Queen, you are the joy of the entire human race.
You are ever loving, gracious and kindly to all.
Truly, you are my highest salvation!

5. *Ambrose of Milan*

St. Ambrose is honored in the Church for a contribution to Christian life and teaching in many areas: biblical,
theological, catechetical, moral, ascetical. He is also recognized for his promotion of hymnody and sacred singing. This particular talent is based on the well-known
story, referred to by Augustine (*Confessions* IX, 7, 15)
regarding the manner in which Ambrose and the faithful
of Milan retained possession of a basilica which the
empress Justina desired for the Arian Christians.
Ambrose and his people kept watch, day and night, in the
church, singing psalms, canticles and hymns, some of
them composed by the bishop, himself. Paulinus, the
earliest biographer of Ambrose notes:

On this occasion, antiphons, hymns, and vigils first began
to be practiced in the Church at Milan, And [sic] the
devotion to this custom remains even to this very day, not
only in the Church, but through almost all the provinces
of the West (Chapter 4, 13).

Although more than twenty liturgical hymns have been
attributed to St. Ambrose, no more than four or five can

definitely be ascribed to him. The two given here are both addressed to Christ.

HYMN FOR THE TIME OF ADVENT[35]
(VENI, REDEMPTOR GENTIUM)

Redeemer of the nations, come,
That we may taste the virgin's fruit
And every age in wonder gaze
On such a birth, worthy of God!
    No earthly father's seed played here,
    But mystic Breath touched virgin womb:
    The Word of God took human form
    And human flesh blossomed divine.
The virgin's womb a burden bears;
A mother still remains a maid.
God lives within this fleshly-shrine;
Banners of grace his presence show.
    See! from his bridal-chamber, now,
    From the high halls of purity:
    A giant, both human and divine!
    A champion shows us how to run!
Proceeding from the Father, God,
To God the Father he returns;
He races to the gates of hell,
Through death, to life, with God to dwell.
    You bear the trophy of Your flesh
    To God eternal, with Him one;
    Strengthen our mortal, earthly frame,
    With conquering grace: the prize you've won.
The cradle where you lie breaks forth
In light that changes night to day;
A light that cannot know dismay
As faith takes up the radiant beam.
    Glory to you, O Virgin-born,

---

[35]This translation has been freely adapted from the Latin, in order to be faithful to the author's thought and to preserve the rhythm of iambic dimeter which Ambrose found conducive to congregational participation.

Our Lord and with the Father, God,
In unity of Spirit, now
And ever, through eternity.

MORNING HYMN
(SPLENDOR PATERNAE GLORIAE)

From out the Father's glory streams
A Splendor; Light from Light, we say;
Light of all Light and Source of Light
And Light enlightening all our days.
    Light more than light: true Son, on us
    Descend in gloom-dispelling rays.
    Let your most Holy Spirit's fire
    Inflame each sense, each heart inspire.
To God the Father, glorious God
Eternal, God of majesty, of grace,
We pay our vows, imploring that
Our sins and guilt be washed away.
    May he direct our acts aright,
    Stay envy's bite and lighten care;
    May he sustain us in this life
    With courage for each day we dare.
Ruler and king of minds is he;
May we in body chaste and free,
Be faithful, so that love's own fire
Preserve us from harmful poison still.
    Then, Christ himself shall be our food
    And faith, the drink to nourish us;
    Joyfully sober, we shall drink
    The Spirit's energizing cup.
O happy day! proceed in joy
To other days. Our innocence
Preserved, no darkness shall we know,
With ardent faith our constant sun.
    The chariot of Dawn appears
    Low in the East. The dawning Day
    Is he: the Son, with Father one,
    Reveals the Father perfectly.

6. *Aurelius Prudentius Clemens*
(A.D. 348-A.D. 405)

Prudentius, as this writer is generally known, is considered by many authors to be the greatest Latin poet of Christian antiquity. He represents that group of Christians who enjoyed the advantages of social prestige and an excellent education. He combined the talents of the literary artist with those of governor in his native Spain. At a time when the Cappadocians, Ambrose and Augustine were engaged in theological discourse on the great Christological mysteries, Prudentius provided another medium, that of poetry, to affirm his fervent Christian faith.

The two following hymns are taken from his *Liber Cathemerinon*, a collection of hymns for different times and activities of every day. In these selections, we also see how the poet attempts to explain certain natural phenomena which remain, in great part, a mystery or are understood in terms of a contemporary explanation which appears, at least, fantastic to us.

VI. A HYMN BEFORE SLEEP[36]

Be with us, Father most high,
Unseen by human, ever;
And Christ, the Father's Word,
And Thou, Spirit-Comforter!
  Thou, God from God eternally
  And God sent forth from Two;
  Yet of this Trinity,
  One only Power; one only Light!
Now ends the labor of the day;
The hour of rest begins, once more.
Slumber, caressing tired limbs,
Announces sleep again.

---

[36]Text: *Prudentius I*, H. J. Thomson, D. Litt., trans. LCL. Cambridge: Harvard University Press, 1949. My translation is an adaptation of the Latin text.

The mind which suffered care,
Anguish and tempestuous storms
Eagerly drinks the potion
That brings forgetfulness, soothes memories.
Throughout the body creeps
The flowing Lethe:
Sorrow and pain depart
In sweet oblivion.
 This is God's law:
 That human frailty
 Might balance toil with pleasure,
 Labor with repose.
But, while the body sleeps,
Wrapped in gentle languor,
And while the heart finds rest,
Refreshment and renewal,
 The spirit is set free
 To roam the heavens,
 Beholding in varied signs
 Secret and hidden things.
Released from care and stress,
The mind speeds to activities,
Fed by its source: the heavens;
Nourished from skies above.
 Thus it fashions, in imitation,
 A multitude of forms
 Among which it wanders,
 Freely, with delight.
But in this land of dreams,
Terror can seize the sleeper.
Knowledge of things to come
Is made known in brilliant light.
 Or else, in contrast,
 Darkness veils the truth.
 The soul, in sadness and fear,
 Wanders through darkness.
The radiant, pulsing light
Makes heaven's secrets known
To one who walks in sinlessness

With soul unsullied.
One who has opened his heart
To foul and wicked deeds
Becomes the prey of dread
And frightening visions.
The patriarch bore witness to this fact
When his interpretation of the dreams
Of royal fellow-prisoners
Proved true, for each.
One was recalled as cup-bearer
To his tyrant-master;
The other, hung on a tree,
Became the prey of vultures.
Next, he brought solace
To the demanding monarch,
Warning of famine to come,
Counseling that provisions be stored.
After, as governor and prince,
He ruled the kingdom in peace,
Sharing the king's own might,
Living in royal splendor.
What deep and secret mysteries
Christ shares with those he loves
When sleep brings untold visions
To the eyes of their heart!
The Master's faithful friend,
The mystic evangelist,
Saw beyond clouds and darkness
Truths formerly unrevealed.
Before his eyes, the Lamb of God,
Bearing the marks of his passion,
Is able to break the seal
And open the book of the future.
In the Lamb's right hand
Flashes the two-edged sword.
It flames and sears like lightening:
Striking twice, with each single blow.
This is the Lamb who
Searches the soul and the body.

The two-edged sword
Is the first and the second death.
   Still, wrath is tempered by kindness:
   How few there are, in the end,
   Who suffer eternal death—
   Even among the wicked!
See how the heavenly Father
Assigns him the throne of judgment.
Learn that the Name he bears
Is held above all other names.
   Christ wages battle with Antichrist,
   Engaged in mortal combat.
   The Lord wins the victory,
   The raging beast is subdued.
That beast, unmasked
And accursed by John,
Seeks to devour the nations,
With insatiable greed.
   That same beast, daring
   To call himself holy,
   Is cast into hell
   By the one, true Christ.
It was John, hero and saint,
Blest with peaceful tranquility,
Whose mind, with prophetic insight,
Pierced these heavenly secrets.
   Not ours, such lofty visions.
   We are bound down each day
   By error and faults,
   By unholy longings for evil.
We seek, in sleep, refreshment,
Renewal of toil-wearied bodies;
We hope for protection
From dark, threatening phantoms.
   Remember this, Christian:
   You have been washed
   In the saving waters of baptism,
   Anointed with holy oil.
When, beckoned by sleep,

You approach an unsullied bed,
Place on your head and your heart
The sign of the cross of salvation.
  Sin is cast out by the cross,
  Darkness and evil, dispelled.
  The mind and the spirit find peace
  Under this sacred sign.
Depart, then, tormenting dreams!
Be gone, deceiver of souls!
Off with your evil phantoms!
Peace to the sleeper!
  Let the false serpent be gone—
  Depart with seductions and fantasies;
  Let no evil beset
  The heart of the sleeper!
Here is the Christ!
Evil, in all forms, be gone!
Before the conquering sign
Let the enemy retreat!
  While the body seeks rest from fatigue,
  Short though the peaceful hours be,
  Even in sleep,
  Let our thoughts be of Christ!

XII: A HYMN FOR EPIPHANY

You who seek Christ,
Lift your eyes to the heavens.
There you will behold
The sign of his eternal glory.
  There is the star
  Whose beauty and light
  Conquer the brilliant sun,
  Proclaiming God's coming to earth in flesh.
This is no servant of the night,
Trailing the moon through her month.
This star owns the sky
And directs the progress of the days.
  The Polar stars, in frigid motion,

Turn back upon themselves;
They never set, but find in clouds
Refuge from our sight.
But, this star does not leave
Nor sink, nor hide:
Its radiance shines through
Every cloud of darkness.
    No need have we of comets,
    Ill-omened orbs; nor meteors
    Lit with burning heat.
    They fade before the star of God.
See, from the depths of Persia,
Doorway of the rising sun,
Magi, expert interpreters of signs,
Behold the majestic star.
    At its shining,
    All other stars recede;
    The Morning Star, itself,
    Hides its resplendent beauty.
"Who is this great ruler?"
Ask the Magi. "He commands the stars;
The heavens stand in awe of him;
Even the light obeys!
    "What glory we behold! The sign
    Of one whose day shall never end.
    Exalted, transcendent, endless in sway,
    More ancient than heaven or hell is he!
"He is that king of the nations,
King, likewise, of the Jews;
Promised of old to Abraham
And to his descendents, forever.
    "That father of all believers,
    Willing to sacrifice his son,
    Received the divine promise
    Of a progeny, as numerous as the stars.
"Here, then, is the flower of David,
Shoot from the root of Jesse;
Coming as blossom on scepter-rod
To rule supreme in the world."

Then did the Magi hasten,
Eyes fixed on the realm above,
To follow that star
Along a pathway of light.
At last, the mystic sign came to rest
Over the head of a Child.
Hanging low, its beams revealed
The One they desired to see.
 Before him, the Magi
 Opened their treasures:
 Royal Gold from the East,
 Frankincense, Myrrh.
Blest Child, read in these gifts
The sign of a threefold dignity,
A triple nature and destiny,
Bestowed by your heavenly Father.
 Gold is the sign of a King;
 Incense from Saba proclaims divinity;
 Myrrh—bitter dust—
 Foretells death and a tomb.
The tomb is the resting place
For a God who suffered and died,
Rising again to life,
Triumphant, breaking death's prism.
 Bethlehem, greatest—not least—of great cities,
 Your honor it was
 To see the birth of Him
 Who, incarnate, brought us salvation.
You nourished and nurtured
The Only Son:
Man, through the Spirit's Power,
God in human flesh.
 Bid by the Father's testament,
 Foretold and witnessed by prophets,
 He enters to claim his kingdom,
 Takes possession of his throne.
His realm embraces everything:
Earth, sky and sea;
Heaven above and hell below;

The wide expanse from east to west.
   And now, the fretful monarch hears
   That One has come—the King of Kings.
   The throne of David will be his;
   The race of Israel to rule.
In frenzy at this word, he cries,
"One to supplant me is already here!
Warriors, go forth with swords unsheathed;
Leave every cradle steeped in blood!
   "Let every male child die.
   Search nurses' bosoms, mothers' breasts;
   Let none be hidden.
   Swords, be reddened by infants' blood!
"No mother of a child in Bethlehem
Is to be trusted.
All will seek escape
To save a new-born male."
   The maddened soldier
   Draws his sword:
   Rent asunder, new-born bodies;
   Lost in anguish, new-born life.
Too small for wounds
So cruelly made, these little ones.
Their throats are smaller
Than the wicked sword.
   Barbarian cruelty that dashes
   Head so small against a stone!
   Innocent brains, unsullied eyes
   Are cast about, in violence.
Here, see a child condemned to death
In swiftly flowing torrent,
As waters of a stream
Snatch breath and life away.
   Hail to you, martyr-blossoms,
   Crushed before life was long;
   You are the roses, cut off too soon,
   By him who pursued the Christ.
First offerings of the world to Christ,
Innocents, holy; a flock of lambs.

Crowns and palms, your playthings;
God's altar, your nursery.
    To what avail this evil deed?
    What good for Herod in his crime?
    The Christ still lives!
    Others are given for his sake.
Children of other mothers died,
Shedding a generation's blood.
The virgin's Son, alone,
Escaped the cruel sword.
    So, Moses, too, was freed
    From Pharoah's foolish whim,
    Prefiguring the Christ,
    Guardian of his people.
We know that law:
No Hebrew mother
Might rear in love
Sons of the womb.
    Here, one faithful midwife,
    In true disloyalty,
    Heeds not the king, and
    Saves the child for future glory.
From boy to manhood grown,
This one is called to priesthood.
To his hands were entrusted
The law, graven on stone.
    In this same man, we see
    Christ, Savior, foretold, prefigured.
    Once the Egyptian master slain,
    Israel's freed from the yoke.
So, too, our Leader
Wounds the enemy,
Freeing us from servitude
To sin, from shades of death.
    Moses led his people,
    Cleansed, through waters sweet,
    Following, the sea behind,
    The pillar's light.
Again, with Israel in battle caught,

Moses stands, arms raised on high.
Prefiguring the cross of Christ,
He sees Amalec subdued.
    Another Jesus—Joshua—
    Prefigures Christ: through wanderings long,
    He leads his men to victory
    And to the Promised land.
Where waters were held back,
He chose and firmly set in place
Twelve stones; again, a type
Of Christ's Apostles Twelve.
    On this Epiphany, the Magi
    Rightly claim to see the promised King:
    Leader of Judah, long foretold
    In lives and deeds of earlier, holy men.
Christ is the King of Judges,
Judge of Kings; ruler of all
Who, then and now, ruled
Church or Temple, new or old.
    Ephraim's sons, Manasses', too,
    And every tribe descended from the brothers twelve,
    Give homage, now, and worship
    To their Lord and God: the Christ.
Worship him, too, do all those sons,
Guilty of fearful deeds
Idolatrous and grim:
Makers of their own gods.
    See, they abandon now
    Idols of stone or wood,
    Metal or any stuff of man,
    For worship true of Christ.
Nations, rejoice! Judaea,
Rome and Greece, Egypt, Thrace, Persia,
Scythia: one is your King!
One is the Ruler of all!
    Let praise arise from every voice:
    Praise from the sheep and the goats;
    Praise from the hearty, the ailing, the dead.
    Christ lives! no longer does death prevail.

7. Romanos Melodos

This author, sometimes referred to as St. Romanus the Singer, has been called the greatest hymn-writer of the entire Church and the most outstanding representative of Greek rhythmic poetry. Ordained a deacon in his native Syria, he served as a member of the clergy in Constantinople, at the Blachernen Church.

The following poem, *On the Nativity*, is an example of his *kontakion*, a metrical sermon chanted to music. It is the only one of eighty extant works which can be authentically attributed to him through a direct witness. In this work, we find the poet's clear affirmation of the two natures in the unity of the one person of Christ. The importance of this theological dimension can be recognized, if we recall that the date of composition of the hymn (*circa* A.D. 518) marks an era when Monophysitism had devastated both the laity and the clergy of Constantinople. The hymn was long popularized by its use at the emperor's table on Christmas day.[37]

PRELUDE

Today the Virgin gives birth
　To the supra-substantial being
And earth provides a cave
　For the Unapproachable One.
Angels with shepherds sing glory
　As Magi follow the Star:
See, it is for us
　That a small child is born:
God from before all ages.
1. Come, let us go to see
　How Bethlehem has opened Eden again.
We have found the delights of that hidden place;
　Let us go, now, to claim once again in a cave
The good things of Paradise.

---

[37]Text in SC 110. French translation and editing by José Grosdidier de Matons.

There has appeared the root never watered
From which forgiveness and pardon have sprung.
    There, rediscovered, the well never dug,
From which David once thirsted to drink.
    There, by this birth, a virgin has quenched
Both Adam's and David's thirst.
    Let us hurry, then, toward that spot
Where a small child is born:
    God from before all ages.
2. The Father of the mother,
        By his own choice,
    Has become the mother's Son.
        The savior of those new-born
    Is, himself, new-born,
        Laid in a manger.
    His Mother, in contemplation,
        Speaks to him:
    "Tell me, my child,
        The way of your coming to be:
    How were you sown in me?
        Before my very eyes
    Is my own flesh!
        I am filled with amazement,
    For, here are breasts ready to nurse you,
        And I have had no husband;
    I see you there in swaddling bands,
        And I am still a virgin.
    It is you who kept the seal unbroken
        When you deigned to enter the world,
    My own little child,
        God from before all ages.
3. "Most high king,
        What is there in common
    Between you and this destitute race?
        Creator of the heavens,
    Why do you come to be
        With creatures of earth?
    Have you lost your heart to a cave?
        Have you fallen in love with a crib?

See, there has not been even a place
　　In the inn for your handmaid.
What do I say? Not one place?
　　Yes, not even a cave—
For this one belongs to others.
　　When Sarah gave birth,
She received a share
　　In measureless land;
I have not even
　　A small plot of ground:
This cave has been borrowed
　　And you have chosen to dwell in it,
My very own small child:
　　God from before all ages."
4. As she murmured these words
　　In prayer to him
Who beholds things unseen,
　　The mother heard voices:
The Magi, seeking the child.
　　"Who are you?" the Virgin queried.
"And who are you, yourself," they replied,
　　"To have given birth to such a child?
Who are your father and mother,
　　Parents of one who is mother and nurse
To an infant without human father?
　　As soon as we saw his star,
We understood a small child had appeared:
　　God from before all ages.
5. "Balaam was right
　　In the meaning he gave to his prophecies:
A star would arise,
　　Outshining, extinguishing
Every oracle and all omens.
　　A star was to shine
And resolve the words of the wise:
　　Their parables, proverbs, enigmas;
A star was to burst forth,
　　More brilliant than this one
We see with our eyes.

for it is he,
   Creator of every star,
      Of whom it is written:
   'Out of Jacob will come a small child,
   God from before all ages.' "

6. When Mary heard these astonishing words,
      She knelt to adore the child of her womb.
   Weeping, she exclaimed:
      "Mighty, my child, mighty is all
   That you have accomplished with my misery.
      Here are the Magi, come from afar to seek you,
   Kings of the Orient seek your face;
      The wealthy of your own people
   Beg to behold you.
      For these, indeed, are your people.
   These men whom you have led to know you,
      You, my own little child,
   God from before all ages.

7. "Since they are your people, my child,
      Grant that they enter under your roof;
   Allow them to see the wealth of your poverty,
      Your priceless destitution:
   The grace and adornment of this dwelling,
      And my own as well, is your own self.
   Give them a sign to come in.
      What matter the poverty here?
   You are the treasure I possess.
      You are the treasure kings come to behold;
   For kings and wise men have learned
      Of your appearance on earth, my little child,
   God from before all ages."

8. Jesus Christ, our true God,
      In secret and unseen manner.
   Touched the soul of his mother and said,
      "Let them enter, who have been led here
   By my Word. For my Word
      Has shone on all those who seek me.
   To the eyes of flesh, it appears as a star;
      For the eyes of the spirit, it is virtue and grace.

Obedient to my command, this star
   Has accompanied the Magi.
Now, unmoving, it fulfills its duty
   By sending its rays
To the birthplace of a little child,
   God from before all ages.
9. "Welcome them, now, holy one,
   Welcome those who have welcomed me;
I am in them as I am in your arms
   And, without leaving your embrace,
I have come here with them."
   Mary opened the door
And welcomed the Magi
   And all who were with them.
She, the impassable door
   Through which, alone, Christ comes,
Opened the door to that company.
   She, who had been opened
Without violation of purity,
   Opened the door.
She opened the door—she, the door,
   Through whom the one Door has come to us,
The little child,
   God from before all ages.
10. The Magi, at once, hastened to enter the room.
   At the sight of Christ, they trembled,
Seeing his mother with her spouse.
   Fearfully, they asked, "Is this the child
Without human ancestry? How is it, Virgin,
   That we find a man in your home?
Your pregnancy brought no reproach,
   But take care, lest you incur blame
If you abide with Joseph.
   Too many are envious of you,
Eager to know where this small child is born,
   God from before all ages."
11. "I will remind you,"
   Mary answered the Magi,
"Why I keep Joseph here:

To confound the wicked,
For he will proclaim
All that he knows about my child.
A holy angel appeared to him
In a dream, to tell him
I had conceived.
During the night,
A fiery vision explained
The cause of his troubles,
Setting his unrest to peace.
That is why Joseph is with me,
To prove that this little child is
God from before all ages.

12. "He makes known clearly all he has heard;
He proclaims surely all he has seen,
In the heavens and on the earth.
He speaks of shepherds and music,
Sung by people of fire and
People of earth, as by one.
He will tell how a radiant star,
Shining ever before you, good Magi,
Led you along a path to this place.
Let us be done with things that are done.
Tell us your story.
Where do you come from?
How have you learned that
a small child was to appear,
God from before all ages?"

13. When she who is radiant with Light
Had thus spoken,
The luminaries from the East answered:
"Would you know whence we have come
To this place? From the land of Chaldea:
There, no one proclaims
'The Lord is the God of gods';
We come from Babylon:
There, no one knows who has created
All we adore.

A spark from the fire of your child
    Has reached into that land,
To snatch us from the Persian Fire
    And lead us here.
We have abandoned and left behind
    The flames that devour all things,
That we might contemplate
    The Fire which refreshes and renews,
The little child,
    God from before all ages.

14. "All is vanity of vanities,
    But no one in our homeland
Sees things that way.
    Some lead astray, others are led;
Thanks and honor to you, O Virgin,
    And to the fruit of your womb,
By whom we have been saved,
    Delivered not only from error,
But from oppression in every land
    Through which we have passed:
From barbarous peoples and foreign tongues,
    Traveling the earth and searching,
Seeking to know, through the light of a star
    Where he was born, the little child,
God from before all ages.

15. But, when we beheld this heavenly lamp,
    We sought through all Jerusalem
And thus fulfilled the prophecy:
    For we have heard that God intended
To sound the city to its depths.
    So did we pass everywhere
With our light,
    Hoping to find the mighty Law.
We failed in our set purpose
    Because the Ark had been taken away
With all its treasured contents.
    The ancient times have now
Been overturned.

All things are made new by this small child,
God from before all ages."

16. "And so," Mary said to the faithful Magi,
"You searched through all Jerusalem,
The city that puts prophets to death?
And how did you pass there unharmed,
Through that place whose eye
Is evil toward all?
How did you escape Herod,
Who breathes murder and not justice?"
They answered, "Virgin,
We did not escape from him,
We eluded him.
Stopping everyone we met,
We asked for the birthplace
Of the little Child,
God from before all ages."

17. When the mother of God heard these words,
She replied, "What did they ask you,
Herod the King and the Pharisees?"
"Herod, first, since
As you have told us,
The leaders of your own people
Had us explain,
Exactly, the time
When this star first appeared;
And when they had learned this,
They acted as if
They knew nothing about it.
They had no desire
To go and behold
Him whom they long sought to know.
For only those who seek truly
Are able to contemplate,
Able to know this little child,
God from before all ages.

18. "Fools!" the Magi exclaimed,
"Thinking us foolish and mad,
Asking us, 'How far have you come?

When did you arrive?
What unknown roads did you travel?'
 But we asked them questions also,
Questions of things they knew well:
 'And you, long ago,
How did you come through the desert?
 He who led you from Egypt
Guided us, even today,
19. Bringing us from distant Chaldea
Straight to himself.
 In the past, by a pillar of fire,
Today, by a star;
 We have been shown a small child
God from before all ages.
["Wherever the star went before us,
 As Moses who carried a rod,
The light of a knowledge divine
 Spread abroad.
In the past, you were nourished on manna,
 Your thirst was quenched from a rock.
We had been fed on his hope,
 Nourished by joy.
We did not think of retracing our steps—
 An impossible route through the desert—
To turn back to Persia.
 We have yearned to adore,
Contemplate and praise this small child,
 God from before all ages'."]
20. So did the Magi speak truthfully.
 The Virgin most holy kept all in her heart;
All was confirmed by the
 Child newly-born:
The inviolate shrine of his Mother,
 Once she had conceived;
The souls and the feet of the Magi,
 Tireless and fresh after their journey.
Not one of them suffered weariness,
 In the manner of Habakuk,
At the time of his visit to Daniel.

He who had spoken to prophets
Was made known also to Wise Men:
    He is the little child,
God from before all ages.
21. After the stories, the tellings,
        The Magi drew near, presents in hand.
    Kneeling before the Gift of all gifts,
        Before the Fragrance of all Perfumes,
    They offered Christ gold and myrrh,
        And, finally, incense.
    "Receive," they exclaimed,
        "This threefold gift,
    As you accept from Seraphim
        The hymn that proclaims you
    Thrice holy!
        Do not reject our offering,
    As you did that of Cain.
        Accept what we bring, rather,
    As you did Abel's gift,
        In the name of her
    Who has given you birth,
        In the name of her
    Of whom you are born,
        Little child,
    God from before all ages."
22. The Virgin, stainless and pure,
        Seeing the Magi there on their knees,
    Carrying gifts splendid and new;
        Beholding the star pointing the way;
    Hearing the songs of the shepherds,
        Offered this prayer to the Lord,
    Creator of these and all living beings:
        "Receive this trinity of gifts,
    My child, and grant three favors
        To the one who has given you birth:
    I pray for the climate and seasons,
        For the fruits of the earth
    And for all who dwell on it.
        Because you have come into this world through me,

Reconcile to yourself all the universe,
    My little child,
God from before all ages.

23. "I am not your mother only,
    Merciful Savior;
It is not in vain that I nourish
    The One who provides milk for all:
I intercede in prayer for all people.
    You have made me the voice of my people,
The honor of my race.
    The earth you have created
Finds its protection in me;
    I am its rampart and strength.
All those you expelled
    From the garden and its delights
Turn their eyes toward me.
    For I am able to lead them
To walk in the ways
    That lead there again.
Let all the universe
    Know and acknowledge
That you have been born of me,
    My small child,
God from before all ages.

24. "Savior, save the world!
    For this you have come.
Restore to fullness
    The work of your hands:
For this you have shone
    Before my eyes,
In the sight of the Magi,
    And through all creation.
See! the Wise Men are here at your feet.
    You revealed to them
The light of your countenance.
    They have brought you gifts,
Useful, beautiful, rare.
    I need these presents, you know,
For I must soon leave for Egypt.

I must flee with you and for you,
My Son, my Guide, my Creator,
   You who have blessed
And enriched me,
   My little child,
God from before all ages."

Chapter Eight

Instructions on Prayer

It is possible to derive a "doctrine" of prayer from the material left us by the early Christian writers and saints. However, another way is open to us, if we would learn more directly from our past lessons on *how to pray.* Here, again, the modes of instruction differ, according to time and place and mentor. We find, once again, the most ancient form of Christian literature, the letter. There is an example of what is called today "journaling." There is an early spiritual conference. In each of the texts cited in the following pages, we can discover the basic principles and foundations for a subsequent doctrine that has continued to nourish and sustain Christians at prayer even until today.

1. St. Augustine: Letter to Proba

The Lady Proba, to whom St. Augustine addressed Letter 130 on prayer, was a member of the noble family of the Anicii Probi. She has, at times, been confused with other women of the noble Anicii family, also named Proba. Her grandmother, it seems, is the Proba who initiated the Christian *cento* tradition, writing the history of salvation out of lines from Vergil, in a style popular in the fourth century. The Proba to whom Augustine wrote was a consecrated widow, the grandmother to whom he refers in his treatise, *De bono viduitatis (On the Excellence of Widowhood)*. She was also known to St. Jerome and St. John Chrysostom.

The letter, written about A.D. 412, witnesses to the relationship between Proba and the bishop of Hippo, whom she consulted as a spiritual guide for herself and for the members of her community—widows and virgins—who settled at Carthage about the year A.D. 410. It is one of the earliest serious instructions on prayer in Christian literature.[38]

Augustine, bishop, servant of Christ and of the servants of Christ, gives greeting in the Lord of lords to Proba, servant of God. (The letter begins with a reflection on the distinction between true and apparent goodness, between the joys of the "true life" and the pleasures of the world, and on the manner in which the Christian is to live by faith.)

"When Christ who is your life, shall appear, then you also shall appear with him in glory." This is the true life which the rich are charged to lay hold on by good works. There is true comfort for the widow who is now desolate, even though she has children or grandchildren, and governs her own house virtuously, dealing with all those for whom she is responsible, so they may place their hope in God. This is her prayer, "For you my soul and my flesh have thirsted, O how many ways! in a desert land, where there is no way, without water." Indeed, this life is a dying life, no matter what finite comforts it affords us, no matter the companions it brings us, no matter what wealth it lavishes on us. I am sure that you known well the uncertainty of such things. Even were they not uncertain, what is their worth, compared to the happiness promised to us?

You asked me for guidance in prayer, but I have said all

---

[38]Cf. *"The Excellence of Widowhood"* in *Saint Augustine*, FOTC 16. 300n.5. This text is adapted from Fathers of the Church, vol. 18, Sister Wilfrid Parson, S.N.D., trans. New York, New York: FOTC 18.

this because you are a widow of wealth and high rank and the mother of a large family who are still with you and who still reverence you. I want you to experience a sense of desolation; to know that you do not yet possess that life where true and certain comfort is found. There, the words of the prophet are fulfilled: "We are filled in the morning with your mercy; we have rejoiced and are delighted all our days. We have rejoiced for the days in which you have humbled us, for the years in which we have seen evils."

In order, then, that you may persevere in prayer night and day until that consolation is yours, do not forget that you abide in desolation, no matter how much you may enjoy the good fortune of earthly riches. The Apostle did not attribute this gift to just any widow. He says, "She that is a widow indeed and desolate has trusted in the Lord and continues in prayers night and day." Note carefully, too, what follows: "But she who lives in pleasure is dead while she is living," for we live in the things which we love, which we seek, which we believe will bring us happiness. What the Scriptures say about riches, therefore, I say to you about pleasure: "If riches abound, do not set your heart on them." If pleasures abound, do not set your heart on them. Do not rely too strongly on the fact that they are not lacking to you, that they serve your satisfaction abundantly, that they seem to flow from a plentiful source of earthly happiness. You must inwardly reject these things and hold them in contempt. You must seek no more of them than is necessary for your bodily health. Because of the necessary activities of this life, good health is not to be despised until "this mortal shall put on immortality." That is our true, perfect and unending health which is not renewed by mortal pleasure when it fails through earthly weakness. It is sustained by heavenly strength. It is made young through eternal incorruptibility. The Apostle himself says, "No one ever hates his own flesh." This seems to be the reason, too, why he rebukes Timothy for too much bodily chastisement and advises him to "use a little wine for his stomach's sake and his frequent infirmities."

These are the pleasures among which a widow is dead, even while she is living, if she lives by them, that is, if her heart clings to them and lingers over the joy they give her. Many holy men and women have been on guard in every way against riches as the very source of pleasure. They have renounced them by distributing them to the poor, thus, in another and better way, storing them up as treasure in heaven. If you feel yourself bound by duty to your family not to follow this course of action, you know what account you must give to God for your use of riches. For, no one "knows what is done in man, but the spirit of a man that is in him." For this reason, we ought not judge anything before the time "until the Lord come; he will bring to light the hidden things of darkness and will make known the counsels of the heart. Then shall everyone have praise from God." If pleasures abound in your life, however, it is part of your duty as a widow not to set your heart on them, lest it wither and die. In order to live, your heart ought to be lifted up on high. Count yourself among those of whom it is written: "Their hearts shall live forever and ever."

You have heard how you are to pray. Hear now what you are to ask in prayer, since this is the point about which you especially wanted my advice. You have been deeply moved by what the Apostle said, "we know not what we should pray for as we ought." You were afraid that you might suffer more harm by praying untruly than by not praying at all. My counsel can be stated briefly: Pray for happiness. This is something we all desire. Even those who live a most wicked, depraved life would never live that way, if they did not imagine that they were actually happy. What else, then, ought we to pray for, except that which the evil as well as the good desire, but which only the good attain?

You will probably ask me next: What is the nature of that happiness? Many philosophical minds have been occupied, and much time has been spent, on that question. Those who have been less successful in answering it are the ones who have paid least honor and given least thanks to its Author. First, then, note whether one should agree with those who place happiness in the following of their own will. God forbid that we should think that true! For what would happen if a person willed to live wickedly? Could we not prove that person to be wretched in proportion to the ease with which his evil purpose was fulfilled? Even those who practise philosophy without recognizing God have rightly repudiated that opinion. For, the most eloquent of them all says: "Look, now, at some others, not exactly philosophers, but fond of debating, who say that all those are happy who live according to their own inclination. But they are wrong, for it is essentially a most unhappy thing to wish for what is not proper. Yet is it not more unhappy to wish to obtain what is not proper than not to obtain what you wish?" What do you think of those words? Were they not spoken by Wisdom herself through the lips of a man? We can then say what the Apostle says of a certain prophet of Crete, whose opinion he accepted: "This testimony is true."

He, then, is happy who has everything he wants, but does not want what is not proper. Accepting that conclusion, note now what we may wish for without impropriety. One person wishes to marry; another, having lost his wife, chooses to live in continence; another, though married, chooses not to enjoy any of the fruits of marriage. Even if anything better is found, here or elsewhere, we cannot say that any of these wish what is not proper; thus, to desire children as the fruit of marriage is obviously to desire life and health to those one has brought forth. Even the chaste widow is commonly absorbed in that wish. Those who reject marriage and no longer wish to beget children still wish life and health to those they have begotten. The chastity of virgins is free from all this care; still, they have all their dear ones for whom they can quite properly wish temporal welfare. But, when we have attained that welfare for ourselves and for those whom we love, shall we be able to say that we are now happy? We may have something which it is proper to wish for, but, if we have nothing else, either greater or better or more to our advantage and personal distinction, we are still far from happiness.

Is it agreed, then, that over and above temporal welfare we may wish for positions of rank and authority for ourselves and our families? Certainly, it is proper for us to wish for these things, for their own sake, but that they may do good by providing for the welfare of those who live under them. It is not proper to covet them out of the empty pride of self-esteem, useless ostentation, or hurtful vanity. Therefore, if we wish for ourselves and our families only what is sufficient of the necessities of life, this sufficiency is not an improper desire in whoever wishes this and nothing more. Whoever does wish more does not wish this and, therefore, does not wish properly. As the Apostle says,"Godliness with contentment is a great gain. For we brought nothing into this world and we can carry nothing out. Having food and clothing, we are content. They that will become rich fall into temptation, the snares of the devil and many unprofitable and hurtful desires. These drown men in destruction and perdition. For the desire of money is the root of all evils. Some who have coveted it have erred from the faith and have entangled themselves in many sorrows." He wished aright and prayed well who said, "Give me not riches or poverty, but only what is necessary for life, lest, being wealthy, I should become a liar and say, 'Who sees me?' or, being needy, might steal and deny the name of my God." Surely, you see that sufficiency is not to be coveted for its own sake, but to provide for bodily health and clothing, in accordance with our personal dignity, making it possible for us to live with others honorably and respectably.

Among all these objects, personal safety and friendship are desired for their own sake, whereas a sufficiency of the necessaries of life is usually sought—when it is properly sought—for the two reasons mentioned above, but not for its own sake. Now, personal safety is closely connected with life itself, and health, and integrity of mind and body. So, too, friendship is not confined by narrow limits; it includes all those to whom love and affection are due. It goes out more readily to some, more slowly to others, but it reaches even our enemies, for whom we are commanded to pray. Thus, there is no one in the human race to whom love is not due, either as a return of mutual affection or in virtue of a share in our common nature. But, those who love us mutually in holiness and chastity give us the truest joy. These are the goods we must pray to keep when we have them, to acquire when we do not have them.

Is this, then, the whole of happiness, and are these all the goods which are comprised in it? Or does truth teach us something else which is to be preferred to all of these? As long as that sufficiency and that personal safety—either our own or that of our friends—is a merely temporal good, it will have to be sacrificed to secure eternal life. Whatever may be true of the body, the soul is certainly not to be considered sane if it does not prefer eternal to temporal goods. For, our temporal life is lived profitably only when it is used to gain merit whereby eternal life is attained. Therefore, all other things which are profitable and properly desired are unquestionably to be referred to that one life by which we live with God and by His life. Inasmuch as we love ourselves in God, if we really love Him, so also, according to another commandment, we truly love our neighbors as ourselves, if, as far as we are able, we lead them to a similar love of God. Therefore, we love God for Himself, but ourselves and our neighbor for His sake. But, even when we live thus, let us not think that we are established in happiness, as if we had nothing left to pray for. How can we find happiness in life when the one incentive to a good life is still lacking to us?

What use is there in spreading ourselves out over many things and asking what we should pray for, fearing that we may not pray as we ought? We should rather say with the Psalmist: "One thing I have asked of the Lord, this will I seek after, that I may dwell in the house of the Lord all the days of my life; that I may see the delight of the Lord, and may visit his temple." In heaven all these days are not accomplished by coming and going; the beginning of one is not the end of another. They are equally without end, since the life of which they are the days has no end. That true Life taught us to pray to attain this blessed life, and not to pray with much speaking, as if we were more likely to be heard, the more words we use in our prayer. He knows, as the Lord Himself said, what is needful for us before we ask Him. For this reason it may seem strange, although He cautions us against much speaking, that He still urges us to pray, since He knows what is needful for us before we ask for it. Yet, He said: "We ought always to pray and not to faint." He used the example of a certain widow who wished to be avenged of her adversary. She petitioned an unjust judge so often that she made him listen to her, not through any motive of justice or compassion, but through weariness of her importunity. In this way we were to be taught how surely the merciful and just God hears us when we pray without ceasing, since the widow, because of her continual petition, could not be treated with contempt even by an unjust and wicked judge. How willingly and kindly God satisfies the good desires of those by whom He knows that others' sins are forgiven, since she who wished to be avenged obtained her desire. There was the man, too, whose friend came to him on a journey. He had nothing to set before him and wished to borrow three loaves from a friend (perhaps the Trinity of one substance is symbolized by this figure). He woke him, as he slept in the midst of his servants, by begging insistently and importunately, so that he gave him as many as he wished. By this we are to understand that if a man, roused from sleep, is forced to give unwillingly in answer to a request, God, who does not know sleep, and who rouses us from sleep that we may ask, gives much more graciously.

The following passage bears on the same thought: "Ask and you shall receive, seek and you shall find, knock and it shall be opened to you. For everyone that asks receives, he that seeks, finds, and to him that knocks it shall be opened. And which man of you if his son ask for bread, will he give him a stone? or if he asks a fish will he give him a serpent? or if he asks an egg will he reach him a scorpion? If you then, being evil, know how to give good gifts to your children, how much more will your Father from heaven give good things to them that ask him?" Of those three things which the Apostle commends, faith is signified by the fish, either because of the water of baptism, or because it remains unharmed by the waves of this world. The Serpent is opposed to it, because it craftily and deceitfully persuaded man not to believe in God. Hope is symbolized by the egg, because the chick is not yet alive but it will be. It is not yet seen but it is hoped for—"for hope that is seen is not hope;"—the scorpion is opposed to it, because whoever hopes for eternal life forgets the things that are behind and stretches himself forth to those that are before, since it is dangerous for him to look backward; he is on guard against the rear of the scorpion, which has a poisoned dart in its tail. Charity is symbolized by bread, for "the greater of these is charity," and among foods bread certainly surpasses all others in value. The stone is opposed to it, because the stony-hearted cast out charity. It may be that these gifts signify something more appropriate. Nevertheless, He who knows how to give good gifts to His children urges us to ask and to seek and to knock.

Since He knows what is needful for us before we ask Him, our mind can be troubled by His acting thus, unless we understand that our Lord and God does not need to have our will made known to him. He cannot but know it. He wishes our desire to be exercised in prayer that we may be able to receive what He is preparing to give. That is something very great, but we are too small and straitened to contain it. Therefore it is said to us: "Be enlarged, bear not the yoke with unbelievers." Thus we shall receive that which is so great, which eye has not seen because it is not color, nor ear heard because it is not sound, nor has it entered into the heart of man, because the heart of man has to enter into it; and we shall receive it in fuller measure in proportion as our hope is more strongly founded and our charity more ardent.

Therefore we pray always, with insistent desire, in that same faith, and hope, and charity. But we also pray to God in words at certain fixed hours and times, so that we may encourage ourselves and take note of how much progress we have made in this desire, and may rouse ourselves more earnestly to increase it. The more fervent the desire, the more worthy the effect which results. That is why the Apostle says: "Desire without ceasing". Let us, then, always desire this of the Lord God and always pray for it. But, because that desire grows somewhat lukewarm by reason of our cares and preoccupation with other things, we call our mind back to the duty of praying at fixed hours. We urge ourselves in the words of our prayer to press forward to what we desire; otherwise, after our desire has begun to grow lukewarm, it then becomes entirely cold and is completely extinguished unless it is frequently rekindled. Consequently, that saying of the Apostle: "Let your petitions be made known to God," is not to be taken in the sense that they are actually made known to God, who certainly knew them before they were uttered. But they are made known to us before God, through our patience, but not before men through our boasting. Or, perhaps they might even be made known to the angels who are with God, so that they may, in a sense, offer our prayers to God and consult Him about them, and bring us back His answer, either openly or secretly, according as they know what He wills, as it befits them to know. Thus, an angel said to Tobias: "And now, when you did pray, you and Sara, I offered the remembrance of your prayer in the sight of the splendor of God."

In view of this, it is not reprehensible or useless to pray at length when one is free, that is, when the obligations of other good and necessary works do not prevent us, although even in those, as I said, we must always pray by that desire of the heart. But, to pray at length does not mean, as some think, to pray with much speaking. Continual longing is not the same as much speaking. For, it is written of the Lord Himself that He passed the night in prayer and that "He prayed the longer." In this He had no other object than to show Himself to us on earth as our ready Advocate, and with the Father as our eternal Benefactor.

It is said that the brothers in Egypt have certain prayers which they recite often, but they are very brief, and are, so to speak, darted forth rapidly like arrows, so that the alert attention, which is necessary in prayer, does not fade and grow heavy through long-drawn-out periods. By this practice they show quite well that, just as this attention is not to be evoked if it cannot be sustained, so, if it can be sustained, it is not to be broken off too quickly. Prayer is to be free of much speaking, but not of much entreaty, if the fervor and attention persist. To speak much in prayer is to transact a necessary piece of business with unnecessary words. But to entreat much of Him whom we entreat is to knock by a long-continued and devout uplifting of the heart. In general, this business is transacted more by sighs than by speech, more by tears than by utterance. For, He sets our tears in His sight and our groaning is not hidden from Him who created all things by His Word and who does not look for human words.

Words, then, are necessary for us so that we may be roused and may take note of what we are asking, but we are not to believe that the Lord has need of them either to be informed or to be influenced. Therefore, when we say "Hallowed be they name," we rouse ourselves to desire that His Name, which is always holy, should be held holy among men also, that is, that it be not dishonored, something which benefits men, but not God. Likewise, when we say "Thy kingdom come," it will come inevitably whether we wish it or not, but we stir up our desire for that kingdom, that it may come in us, and that we may deserve to reign in it. When we say "Thy will be done on earth as it is in heaven," we ask of Him that obedience for ourselves, so that His will may be done in us as it is done in heaven by His angels. When we say "Give us this day our daily bread," by "this day" we mean "at this time," when we either ask for that sufficiency, signifying the whole of our need under the name of bread, which is the outstanding part of it, or for the sacrament of the faithful, which is necessary at this time for attaining not so much this temporal as that eternal happiness. When we say "Forgive us our debts as we also forgive our debtors," we warn ourselves both what to ask and what to do that we may deserve to obtain mercy. When we say "Lead us not into temptation," we warn ourselves to ask not to be deprived of His help, not to consent to any temptation through deception, not to yield through tribulation. When we say "Deliver us from evil," we warn ourselves to reflect that we are not yet in that happy state where we shall suffer no evil. And the fact that this petition is placed last in the Lord's Prayer shows plainly that the Christian, beset by any kind of trouble, utters his groans by means of it, pours out his tears in it, begins, continues and ends his prayer by it. By these words it was fitting to recall the truths thereby implied to our mind.

For, whatever other words we may say, whatever words out fervor utters at the beginning of a petition to define it, or follows up afterward to intensify it, we say nothing that is not found in this prayer of the Lord, if we pray properly and fittingly. But, whoever says anything in prayer which does not accord with this Gospel prayer, even if the prayer is not of the forbidden sort, it is carnal, and I am not sure it ought not to be called forbidden, since those who are born again of the Spirit ought to pray only in a spiritual manner.

(Here, Augustine expands the theme developed in his brief commentary on the Lord's Prayer, by a series of examples of petitions which are implicitly contained in the words taught us by Jesus.)

Now, you know, I think, not only the nature of your prayer, but its object, and you have learned this, not from me, but from Him who has deigned to teach us all. Happiness is what we must seek and what we must ask of the Lord God. Many arguments have been fashioned about the nature of happiness, but why should we turn to the many arguments? Brief and true is the word in the Scripture of God: "Happy is the people whose God is the Lord." That we may belong to that people and that we may be able to attain to contemplation of Him and to eternal life with Him, "the end of the commandment is charity from a pure heart and a good conscience, and an unfeigned faith." Among those same three, hope is put for a good conscience. "Faith, therefore, and hope and charity," lead the praying soul to God, that is, the believing and hoping and desiring soul who attends to what he asks of the Lord in the Lord's Prayer. Fasting and abstinence from other pleasures of carnal desire—with due regard for our health—and especially alms-giving are great helps to prayer, so that we may be able to say: "In the day of my trouble I sought God with my hands lifted up to him in the night, and I was not deceived." (At this point, Augustine takes up Paul's affirmation in

Romans 8:26, "We know not what we should pray for as we ought." He attempts to explain this verse, repeating some of the earlier themes he has developed in the letter.)

Think over all this, and if the Lord gives you any other idea on this matter, which either has not occurred to me or would be too long for me to explain; strive in your prayer to overcome this world, pray in hope, pray with faith and love, pray insistently and submissively, pray like the widow in the parable of Christ. For, although the obligation of prayer rests on all His members, that is, all who believe in Him and who are joined to His Body, as He taught, a more particular and more earnest devotion to prayer is enjoined on widows, as we see in His Scripture. There were two women with the honored name of Anna: one married, who gave birth to holy Samuel; the other a widow, who recognized the Saint of saints when He was still an infant. The married one prayed with grief of soul and affliction of heart, because she had no sons. In answer to her prayer Samuel was given to her, and she offered him to God as she had vowed in her prayer to do. It is not easy to see how her prayer agrees with the Lord's Prayer, except, perhaps, in those words, "Deliver us from evil," because it seemed no slight evil to be married and to be deprived of the fruit of marriage, when the sole purpose of marriage is the begetting of children. But, note what is written of the widow Anna, that "she departed not from the temple, by fasting and prayers, serving night and day." And the Apostle, as I said above, speaks in the same tenor: "But she that is a widow indeed, and desolate, hopes in the Lord, and continues in prayers night and day." When the Lord exhorted us to pray always and not to faint, He told of the widow whose continual appeal brought a wicked and impious judge, who scorned both God and man, to hear her cause. From this it can easily be understood how widows, beyond all others, have the duty of applying themselves to prayer, since an example was taken from widows to encourage us all to develop a love of prayer.

But, in a practice of such importance, what characteristic of widows is singled out but their poverty and desolation? Therefore, insofar as every soul understands that it is poor and desolate in this world, as long as it is absent from the Lord, it surely commends its widowhood, so to speak, to God its defender, with continual and most earnest prayer. Pray, then, as the widow praised by Christ, not yet seeing Him whose help you ask, however wealthy you may be; pray like a poor woman, for you have not yet the true wealth of the world to come, where you need fear no losses. And, although you have sons and grandsons and a numerous family, pray as a desolate widow, as was explained above, for all temporal things are uncertain, even though they last, for our consolation, to the end of this life. But, for your part, if you seek and relish the things that are above, if you sigh for the things that are eternal and certain, as long as you do not possess them, even though all your family are safe and devoted to you, you ought to look on yourself as desolate. So also should your most devout daughter-in-law, as well as the other holy widows and virgins gathered safely under your care. For, indeed, the more religiously you conduct your household, the more earnestly should all of you persevere in prayer, free of preoccupation with worldly affairs, except inasmuch as family affection requires.

Surely, you will also remember to pray attentively for me, for I do not wish you, out of regard for the position which I occupy, to my own peril, to deprive me of a help which I recognize as necessary. By Christ's household, prayer was made for Peter, prayer was made for Paul; you rejoice to belong to His household, and there is no comparison between my need of the help of fraternal prayers and that of Peter and Paul. Vie with each other in prayer, in a mutual and holy rivalry, for you will not vie against each other, but against the Devil, who is the enemy of all the saints. Let each one of you do what she can in fasting, in watching and in every bodily chastisement, all of which is a help to prayer. If one can do less, let her do what she can, so long as she loves in another what she does not do herself because she cannot. Thus, the weaker will not hold back the stronger, and the stronger will not press the weaker. You owe your conscience to God, "owe no man of you anything but to love one another." May the Lord hear your prayer, "Who is able to do more abundantly than we desire or understand."

2. Paulinus of Pella: A Poem of Thanks

The name, Paulinus, is not uncommon on the roster of early Christian writers. The author in whom we are interested was born as Pella, in Macedonia, probably toward the end of the year A.D. 376. When the child was nine months old, his family moved to Carthage, where his father exercised the office of proconsul of Africa. By the age of three, Paulinus had been in Rome, Gaul and Bordeaux, the home of his ancestors. There seems strong evidence to support the claim of some scholars that Paulinus was the grandson of Ausonius, Roman poet and rhetorician.

The following lines are excerpts from the *Eucharisticos*, an autobiographical poem published in A.D. 459. The work seems to have been based on a personal journal in which the author had recorded the significant events of his life. As the title of the poem indicates, Paulinus intended this work to be an expression of gratitude to God for the graces received during eighty-three years of life.

While this type of autobiography was completely unknown in Gaul, it seems that Paulinus was inspired by the *Confessions* of St. Augustine to give expression to his faith and thanksgiving to God, rather than to provide a detailed account of his life.

As an example of instruction on prayer, the following passages demonstrate both a method of theological reflection on personal experience and an expression of a prayer of thanksgiving for the guidance and protection of divine Providence in one Christian's life.

A POEM OF THANKS BY PAULINUS[39]

Preface

I know that there are some famous persons who have left to posterity an account of their daily actions, written for the purpose of assuring immortality to their prestige and glory.

---

[39]SC 209.

The outstanding qualities of these authors place them as far from me as does distance in time. Thus, my intention in writing this little work on a similar topic in no way can be compared to theirs. I have accomplished no achievements striking enough to merit the least glory; nor do I have enough confidence in my ability as a writer to dare to set myself up easily as a rival to any author at all.

However, I have no problem in admitting that I am sure that the divine mercy has led me to seek consolation in a manner fitting to an old man whose conscience is at peace and whose heart entertains a devout plan. The peace has come after a long period during which I languished under the weight of sadness, the result of forced inactivity. The plan comes from my conviction that, beyond any doubt, I owe my entire life to God. I have wanted, then, to show that every action of my life has been consecrated to his service. For this, I thought of reflecting on the years his kindness and goodness have granted me and of composing in his honor a little work of thanksgiving, based on what I have recorded in my journal.

I am certain that the Lord's merciful goodness has been shown me, because even in my infancy I knew those passing joys that are granted to human beings. I know, too, that his loving Providence has also been graciously manifest toward me. In the tempered sufferings which came from incessant trials of one kind or another, Providence clearly taught me salutary lessons. First, I ought not be too strongly attached to this life's happiness, fleeting as I know it to be. Secondly, I ought not be too greatly disturbed by life's evils, in the midst of which, experience has taught me, the loving help of God is able to assist me.

Therefore, if ever my work should fall into the hands of any person, that individual must realize from the title that this little meditation is dedicated to the omnipotent God. It was meant to occupy my leisure hours rather than provide entertainment for the free time of other people. Indeed, I much prefer that this witness to my devotion, whatever its value, please God rather than be recognized as a mediocre poem by scholars.

Nevertheless, if, by chance, a more interested reader with enough leisure would follow the unfolding of my story and the recital of my well-tried experience, I ask one thing. If that reader find in my actions or even in my verse something, or anything, that can be applauded, I request that it, nonetheless, be cast into oblivion—without condemnation—rather than be transmitted to the judgment of posterity.

(11. 1-20)
As I give myself to the task of writing the story
Of years now gone by; of describing the course of events
Lived through the days of time past until now;
I come to the end of a life whose term is uncertain.
I pray you, omnipotent God, in your care for me, help me.
If this work finds favor with you, inspire me, favor me.
Grant that this writing, my offspring, be born;
Grant that my wish be fulfilled so that, thanks to your help
I may recount all your blessings.
To you do I owe every moment of life, from the first,
When I breathed in the luminous air of existence.
Protected by you, I have passed through the tempests and storms
Of a world, hostile and fickle.
The twelfth week of my years has already passed;
Since then, I have counted six burning seasons of sun,
Summer's heat; as many of ice-frozen winters.
These are your gift to me, O my God. You renew
The cycle of years which have passed; you bring back
The course of time, making it retread the path once taken.
May I, then, be granted the time and the favor
To celebrate all your goodness, to sing your gracious deeds,
In a poem whose language bears witness to all that I feel
Of thanksgiving to you. This thanks, though concealed in our heart,
Is already known to you. I do not doubt this;
But my voice, aware of the secret, would snatch it out
From the silent depths of my soul and let flow the source
Of my hopes and desires, which now pour forth in abundance.

(Paulinus reviews the first years of his life; his childhood at Bordeaux, his study of Socrates, Homer and Vergil. His earliest difficulty seems to have been with the Greek language. "Bilingual study," he states, "is suitable for superior minds....I realize now that it drained the meager resources of my intelligence." He expresses the regret that his parents, who saw to his early Christian initiation and formation, did not encourage him to persevere in following a religious vocation in his youth.)

(11. 100-112)
But now, I am able to see the worth of my life;
The destiny of the path followed was true to your plans;
More surely, thus, has it wrought my salvation.
Eternal, omnipotent God, ruler of all,
I am a sinner, renewed by your life-giving grace.
I am in debt for your graces, greater by far
Than any great faults of which I have been guilty.
For, all that I may have committed in actions faulty, forbidden,
In wandering astray through dissolute periods of life,
I know is forgiven entirely because of your goodness.
I know I have failed and I come to your justice seeking for mercy.
If I have ever avoided more serious sins;
If I have been kept from guilt even greater,
It is only because of the grace of my God,
Of you, who have saved and preserved me.

(Paulinus continues to relate the events of his life. At the age of fifteen, he was stricken by a serious illness, perhaps brought on by his intense efforts to please his parents through excelling in his studies. In order to favor his return to health, his parents indulged his every whim and desire: a magnificent horse; a noble riding master; a superb dog and falcon; everything needed for hunting. There were other attractions, too. He claims never to have seduced a woman against her will nor to have dishonored another man's wife. His liaisons were never with a free woman, but only with the slave-girls of his own household. "I preferred to be accused of a fault rather than a crime," he writes, "and I lived in fear of losing my good reputation." A son was born to one of the women he knew, but the infant died soon after birth. This event seems to have led him away from what might have become a life of debauchery. He married at the age of twenty, devoting himself to the serious business of the responsibilities that came to him, at that time.)

(11. 202-218)
Above all, I sought a modest and restful existence,
Far from ambitious endeavors
I needed a well-planned dwelling with rooms, large and attractive,
Whatever the time of the year; a generous table, bearing choice foods;
Servants many and youthful; beautiful furniture,
Sufficient in number and suited for various uses;
Silverware, worth more in price than in weight;
Artisans gifted with talents and trades,
Ready to bring to completion whatever command I might give them.
Stables I had, filled with horses well-cared for,
And wonderful chariots, designed for travel in comfort and safety.
However, I sought less to increase my possessions
Than to conserve them; I had no desire for greater wealth
Nor did I covet honors; what I sought was the good life,
On condition that I might have it without a great cost
And, always, preserve the integrity of my good name.

(The attachment of Paulinus to his parents is broken by the death of his father. Increased wealth brought added cares and his property was pillaged by the Goths, who had been living peacefully in Bordeaux. A long period of harrassment at the hands of the barbarians and betrayal by friends followed.)

(11. 431-450)
But, if I judge rightly, O Christ, I must rejoice:
My destiny has been such as you have willed.
And now, you promise me goods that surpass by far
Those in which I rejoiced in the days when I held them,
Sure that your kindness enriched me, met my desires.
In those days, my home was radiant with splendor,
While many pleasures and dazzling honors
Adorned those who surrounded me; the support of a crowd
of guests
Knew no lesser prestige. Today, I regret
The value I placed on those goods, so soon to vanish.
At last, in old age, I can judge justly, knowing
It was for my good that all was taken from me.
After the loss of these earthly, perishable riches,
I learned to seek, rather, those which can last forever.
My learning was late, well I know! but no time
Is too late for you, my God, whose existence knows no end
And whose mercy is not less infinite.
You alone know how to bring help in ways beyond our
knowing;
You anticipate the desires of all those who come
In great numbers before you; even before we ask,
You give assurance that good things will be ours,
Beyond the extent of our asking.
When we know not what we should seek for ourselves,
You refuse to grant requests beyond number.
But, to those who know how to prefer your gifts
To the things they desire, you are eager to grant
All that works to their good.

> (When he was about forty-five years of age, Paulinus
> experienced a deep and radical conversion which led him
> to aspire to the monastic life. Realizing, however, his
> responsibility for two sons, a mother, a mother-in-law
> and a wife, not to mention the servants of his household,
> he chose, instead, to live according to an ascetical rule,
> under the direction of "holy persons who assisted me by
> their counsels."

Other trails befell this faithful Christian, the most painful of which was the loss of all the members of his family
in death. Loss of property and possessions followed.
When he was about sixty years of age, he retired to
Marseilles, there to live in simplicity, humility and poverty. One of his embarrassments, at this time, was the
assistance brought him by wealthy acquaintances. He
found himself torn between accepting this human aid and
entrusting himself totally to Providence.)

(11. 564-616)
However, you did not allow me to be overcome for long
By the uncertainties of that kind of life.
Without my asking it, my God, you judged well
To bring solace and comfort to me, without delay.
You do not cease to care for me with remedies
To strengthen me in my old age, when I grow feeble
Because of past illnesses.
Now, you have renewed my vigor; you have shown me
That I must, absolutely, no longer hope for
Revenue from my patrimony. I have lost the ownership
Of even those goods which I possessed in my poverty in
Marseilles,
Only because they were pledged to others on whom I
depended.
Then, inspired by you, a Goth whom I did not know
Offered to buy a small piece of property
Which formerly had been mine; on his own, he sent me the
money.
It was surely not the true worth of the land,
But I received with joy, I admit, that sum
Thanks to which I could shore up the remains of a ruined
fortune
And prevent my pride from being hurt anew.

In the joy that has come with this magnificent favor,
I am once again in debt to you, omnipotent God.
Once again, I owe you thanks which must surpass
All the gratitude I have ever expressed to you in the past,
and more.

This entire work which I have written is filled
With the solemn proclamation of my thanks.
Even though my verbosity has caused it to run this long,
And even now calls for an end to its course,
My devotion is inexhaustible; I cannot cease
From rendering to you, O Christ, the homage that is your
due.
I know that there is one good alone
That I must possess and I desire it with all my heart.
It is this: that, in every place, without exception,
And at all times, without excluding any,
I may be able to celebrate you by my words
And, in my silence, to hold you present in my mind.
Therefore, since I owe myself and all that is mine
To you, most good and loving God,
I began this work with you and, having reached the end,
I also consecrate its conclusion to you.
I have often prayed fervently to you. I implore you now,
More ardently still.
In the life I lead now, as an old man,
I see nothing more fearful than death itself.
It is not easy for me to discern
What preference I ought to have in this regard.
Furthermore, whatever your will may be for me
At that last moment, grant me, I pray, a soul
Unshaken by any evil and confirm me by the gift
Of your own power. In this way,
Since I have lived so long a time submissive to the laws
That are acceptable to you; since I strive to reach
The salvation you have promised, grant that I may not more
greatly fear death,
To whom every age is subject, at a time
When old age brings me closer to it.
Grant that, in the apprehension of the dangers of an uncer-
tain life,
I may not be tormented by the fear of all those evils
Which I know I can avoid, if you, O God, protect me.
Whatever is reserved for me, as my life comes to an end,
May the hope of beholding you, O Christ,

Bring me sweet comfort. May all the doubts of anguish
Be dispelled by the trusting certainty,
No matter where I am, that, as long as I am in
This mortal body which is mine, I belong to you
To whom all things belong.
May I know surely, then, that once I have been freed
From all restraints of earth,
I shall find life anew
Somewhere in your body.

3. John Cassian:
First Conference of Abbot Isaac on Prayer

John Cassian is not frequently counted among the
Fathers of the Church, although he lived in the patristic
era and was ordained to the diaconate by the great John
Chrysostom. John Cassian is surely respected as a
"father" of Christian and monastic spirituality, having
learned from the ascetics in the deserts of Egypt and from
his own experience as Abbot of the monastery he
founded in Marseilles (A.D. 415).

The following text presents excerpts from *Conference
IX*, in the work, *Collationes*. It is based on the first
conference of Abbot Isaac on prayer. While the instructions were intended, primarily, for a monastic community, the following selection will be readily recognized as a
message which can be addressed to all Christians.

II.[40]...The entire edifice of virtues taken together exists for
one purpose only, that is, that we may attain perfection in
prayer. Without this crowning achievement, by which the
separate parts within us are brought together into a unified
whole, there will be neither a firm foundation nor stability
to our prayer. Indeed, without the virtues, the constant
tranquility of prayer we are discussing is neither acquired

[40]Text: SC 54.40, ed., Dom E. Pichery; CSEL 13, ed., Petscheniz

nor fully realized. On the other hand, the virtues, which are the basis of prayer, will never reach their own perfection apart from it.

For this reason, it would be absurd to undertake, from the start—without any preliminary explanations—an adequate discussion of prayer in all its fullness. That presupposes the practice of all the virtues. We have no choice but, first of all, to examine in order the obstacles to be removed and the necessary preparations to assure success in our venture. Enlightened by the gospel parable, we must first of all calculate the cost of our enterprise and then diligently assemble all that is needed for the construction of this lofty spiritual tower!

I repeat: even when the materials have been readied, they would be of no use without the preparatory labor. In themselves, they could not support the exalted summit of perfection. We must, therefore, undertake the task of ridding ourselves of all our vices and of clearing our soul of the debris and ruin caused by our passions. Then, we must lay the solid foundations of simplicity and humility on the good, firm ground of our hearts, so to speak, or rather, on the solid rock of which the gospel speaks. There, the tower which is to be raised with our virtues may be surely established and, confident in its own solidity, may reach to the highest heavens.

If this tower is constructed on such a foundation, it will not crumble or fall. Let the storms of passion and the violent torrents of persecution come; let hostile powers and fierce tempests rage and unleash their fury. I say that the impact will not even weaken it.

III. In order to arrive at the fervor and purity which ought to characterize it, prayer demands of us complete fidelity on several points.

First of all, we must totally suppress all anxiety concerning the flesh. Then, concerns and more, the memory even, of every matter that occupies or absorbs our interest must be absolutely dismissed. After this, we ought also to renounce slander, idle conversation, gossip and foolish speech. Above all, strike at the root of anger or sadness. Tear out unmercifully the core of concupiscence of the flesh and love of money.

Once these vices and their companions—even those which escape the human eye—have been entirely removed and destroyed; after the purification we have described has been begun and we are on the way to purity, simplicity and innocence, we can lay the unshakable foundations of a deep humility. By this, the tower will be upheld and its lofty summit will reach to the heavens. Then, we can construct the spiritual house of the virtues. Finally, withhold your soul from seeking escape in wayward or flighty thoughts, so that you may thus begin to ascend, gradually, to the contemplation of God and of spiritual realities.

Indeed, everything we have in our minds before we begin the time of prayer is inevitably re-presented to us by the memory, while we pray. We must seek to be before prayer what we want to be and to do in prayer. The attitudes and thoughts of our heart during prayer depend on the state we were in as we begin to pray. As we kneel to pray, the same actions, words and feelings we have known are reborn from our imagination. Depending on what they were before we began to pray, they may arouse in us anger or sadness. Or again, we may find ourselves reliving the desires and concerns that assailed our heart. We laugh aloud—I am ashamed to say—at the thought of some frivolous word or deed that comes to mind. Our thoughts take flight in daydreaming and wool-gathering.

All the strange ideas we would be free of during the time of prayer must thus be banished with a care drawn from the temple of our heart before we begin to pray. Then we shall be able to heed the admonition of the Apostle: "Pray without ceasing!" and, again: "In every place, raise clean hands to heaven, without anger or contention!" We, however, shall remain forever incapable of this prayer, if our soul is not cleansed from every stain of vice and devoted to virtue as its very own, so as to be nourished by the constant contemplation of the omnipotent God.

IV. The soul might easily be compared to fine down or to a delicate feather. If it remains unsoiled by moisture, it rises almost spontaneously in the air. When, on the contrary, it is wet or dampened by any liquid at all, it becomes weighted down! Farewell to ascent and flight! Its natural mobility is no longer a source of delight. The weight of its wetness brings it down to the ground.

So is it with the soul. If vices and worldly cares do not weigh it down and if passion does not soil it, it rises, one might say, by the innate privilege of its purity. At the lightest breath of spiritual meditation, it mounts towards the heights and, leaving the things of this world behind, it rises to those which are celestial and invisible.

It is then, indeed, to us, specifically, that the Lord speaks in the gospel when he says, "Take care that your hearts be not weighed down with dissipation and drunkenness and the cares of this life!" Do we want our prayers to reach the heavens? Let us seek to free our hearts from every earthly vice; let us purify ourselves from slavery to passion, so that we may possess the natural subtlety proper to our soul. Then, our prayer will be free from the dead weight of the vices. Then, it will ascend even to God.

V. Let us, however, pay attention to the causes the Savior identified for the soul's heaviness. He did not speak of adultery, fornication, homicide, blasphemy, or theft. Everyone knows these evils are the cause of death and damnation. Rather, he named dissipation, drunkenness and the cares or concerns of the present age. . . .

These three vices, literally understood, weigh down the soul who gives herself to them. They separate her from God and bring her down to the earth. It is, nonetheless, easy for us to avoid them, especially those of us who are far from the world because of distance and the way of life we have chosen. We have no occasion whatever of being captivated by the care of visible things nor by excesses in drinking and eating.

But there is another kind of dissipation which is no less disastrous for us. There is spiritual drunkenness, more difficult to avoid. There is another sort of wordly care and concern. And even when we have entirely renounced all our possessions; when we live in complete abstinence from food, drink and a comfortable way of life; when we have freed ourselves from the very essence of our cares and concerns, we can still be often enough caught in their snares.

It is of us, then, that the prophet speaks, when he says: "Awaken, you who are drunk, but not with wine [Joel 1:5(LXX)]." And still another writes,

> Daze yourselves, and be dazed,
> Blind yourselves, and be blind,
> You who are drunk, though not with wine,
> You who reel, though not with strong drink! (Isa.29:9)

The wine which causes this drunkenness can be only "the venom of dragons," according to the prophet. Just see the root from which it comes: "Their vine comes from the stock of Sodom, and from the fields of Gomorrah" (Deut 32:32). Would you know still better the fruit of this vine and the produce of these shoots? "Their grapes are poisonous grapes; bitter clusters are theirs."

Yes, if we are not completely purified of all vices; if we have not been freed from our passions, in vain shall we have renounced excess in wine and abundance of food. Our hearts will carry the burden of an even more dangerous drunkenness and gluttony....

VIII. I am convinced that it is impossible to distinguish all the forms of prayer, without a great purity of heart and extraordinary graces from the Holy Spirit. The number and kinds of prayer are as great as the various states and dispositions to be found in one soul; rather, in all souls together. I am aware that my hardness of heart makes it impossible for me to discern them all. Nevertheless, I shall try to describe them, for better or worse, within the limits of my poor experience.

Prayer changes at every moment, according to the degree of purity the soul has reached, in keeping with its actual dispositions, whether they be due to foreign or spontaneous influences. It is certain that prayer is never the same at all times for anyone. We pray in a different manner when our heart is light and when it is burdened with grief or despair. Our prayer is one way when we are caught up in the ecstasy of the supernatural life; another, when we are beseiged by violent temptations. When we beg forgiveness for our faults, our prayer is not one of petition for grace, virtue, healing from a sinful habit. One is the prayer of compunction inspired by the thought of hell and the final judgment; another, the prayer from a heart burning with desire and the hope of future blessings. In adversity and peril, in peace and security; inundated by light from the revelation of the mysteries of heaven or paralyzed by sterility in virtue and dryness in thought: in each distinct and discrete manner do we pray.

IX. I have spoken above of different prayers. My words were too few for what the extent of such a subject might demand. I had to measure my discourse to the time available to us as well as to the lack of insight on the part of my limited intelligence and my earth-bound heart. Now, I am faced with a still more serious problem: that of describing in detail the various species of prayer.

The Apostle identifies four: "I urge that supplications, prayers, intercessions and thanksgivings be made." This division is not futile; we can have no doubt of that. We must, then, first seek to know the meaning of these words: supplication, prayer, intercession, thanksgiving. We shall then see whether all four species are to be used at the same time when we pray, so that they are invoked everywhere and always. Or, is it appropriate to offer them separately, each in turn? Ought we to offer, at one time, supplications; at another, prayers; intercessions, today; thanksgiving, tomorrow? Or rather, must one person offer supplications to God, while another offers prayers? A third intercedes and still another gives thanks—so that each individual prays according to age, fervor and zeal?

X. First of all, then, what is the exact meaning of these terms? That is our first question. What difference is there between prayer, supplication and intercession? In the second place, ought these acts occur separately or together? Thirdly, is there some special teaching for the benefit of the faithful in the very order in which the Apostle, on his own authority, lists these words? Or is the sequence to be looked upon in a more simple manner, with the idea that the Apostle had no particular intention in mind? This last idea, frankly, seems absurd to me. I cannot believe that the Holy Spirit spoke through the mouth of the Apostle in a casual way, without motivation. We are now going to take each of these species individually, in the order indicated and consider them as God gives us grace to do so.

XI. "I urge you, above all, to make supplications." A supplication is the cry, the prayer of a sinner touched by the grace of repentance, imploring pardon for his past and present sins.

XII. Prayer is the act by which we offer or vow something to God. The Greeks called it, "*euchē*, that is, "vow.". . . This is how we fulfill the precept to pray:

We pray when we renounce the world and solemnly commit ourselves to die to the pursuits and lifestyle of the world, in order to serve the Lord with all the ardor of our soul. We pray when we commit ourselves to despise the glory of this age and to trod underfoot all earthly riches, in order to adhere to the Lord with a contrite heart and a poor and humble spirit. We pray when we vow forever to God perfect chastity of body, unchanging patience and commit ourselves to tear out of our heart the roots of anger and that sadness which brings death.

If we are unfaithful to our promises and allow ourselves to be overcome by laxity, returning to our former vices, we shall be accountable for our prayers and our vows. It will be said of us: 'It is better not to make vows than to make but not keep them." Or, as the Greek expresses it: "It is better not to pray than to pray and be unfaithful."

XIII. Intercessions come in the third place. These are the prayers we offer for others in the fervor of our minds, whether the petitions are for those who are dear to us, for peace in the world or, to borrow the Apostle's words, "for all humanity, for kings and all who are in high positions."

XIV. Then, in the fourth place, we consider thanksgiving. When the soul recalls past blessings received from God and considers those with which she is now graced; or when she looks toward the future, in expectation of the infinite reward prepared for those who love God, she is caught up in inexpressible raptures of gratitude. It even happens that such considerations lead her to pray with greater outpourings of thanks. For, in contemplating in purity of mind all that is reserved for the saints in the life to come, she feels impelled to pour herself out before God in effusive acts of gratitude, caught up in a joy beyond measure.

XV. These four species are the fruitful sources of prayer, properly so-called. Experience has taught us that supplication is the daughter of repentance. Prayer (the "vow") is born in a pure conscience of fidelity to one's offerings and the fulfillment of one's vows. Intercession flows from the ardor of love. Thanksgiving, fruit of consideration of the blessings of God, his majesty and his goodness, often breaks forth in fervent prayers, all flame and fire.

It is certain, furthermore, that all of these prayers are useful, if not indispensable, to each of us. We shall find the same person, in different states or according to varying circumstances, offering supplications, prayers, intercessions, and thanksgiving.

However, the first form of prayer seems to be more particularly suited to beginners who are still beset by vices and pursued by remorse. The second is, rather, for those who are making progress, seeking virtue and moving steadily toward the heights. The third seems appropriate for those whose life corresponds fully to their commitments and who, beholding the frailty of a neighbor, feel impelled in charity to intercede for others. The fourth, finally, is the prerogative of those who have uprooted from their hearts the painful thorn of remorse. They live, now, in tranquility, considering in purity of heart the abundant blessings and mercies which the Lord has showered on them in the past; the graces with which he continues to bless them and the glories which he prepares for them in the life to come. Their hearts are enflamed, transported, in the ecstasy of a prayer of fire which human words are not able to express.

It does happen, however, that even one who reaches this final state of true purity of heart and who abides, rooted, in it engages, at the same time, in all forms and species of prayer. She is carried from one to the other by a consuming, devouring flame. She pours herself out in living, pure prayers which the Holy Spirit utters within us, in our name, with unspeakable groanings to God. She conceives and lets pour out from her heart in one single instance of silent, effusive prayer so many affections and sentiments that she would be incapable of expressing—or, even, imagining—them at any other moment.

It also happens that one can attain to this intense, pure prayer, in some degree, even in the first and lowest state as a consequence of meditation on the last judgment. While the soul trembles with fright and terror at the thought of the terrible trial and chastisement in store for the guilty, she feels, at that moment, deeply moved by repentance. Out of the abundance of her supplication there comes a surge of enthusiasm of spirit. She is completely possessed by this sentiment no less than one who, in the splendor of purity, contemplates the blessings of her God and, at the sight, is borne aloft in joy and ecstatic delight. This is possible to a beginner because, according to the words of the Lord, she begins to love more, realizing that she has been forgiven more.

XXXV. We ought to be particularly careful to follow that evangelical precept which tells us to enter into the secret of our room and close the door when we pray to the Father.

This is how we can follow this admonition.

We pray in our room when we withdraw our heart entirely from the tumult and noise of worldly thoughts and concerns and, in a sort of secret tête-à-tête of sweet intimacy, make known all our desires to the Lord.

We pray with the door closed when we pray with closed lips, beseeching the One who takes no heed of words, but who reads our hearts.

We pray in secret when we speak to God with our heart and the attention of our soul only, making known our needs to him alone, so that even the hostile powers of the enemy cannot tell the nature of our requests. This, in fact, is the reason for the deep silence we ought to keep when we pray. We ought not only avoid distracting those around us by our whisperings and groanings, obliging them to deal with obstacles in their prayer. We ought also hide the object of our petitions from our enemies who seek to increase their assaults when we pray. By so doing, we fulfill the precept, "Guard the doors of your mouth from her who lies in your bosom."

XXXVI. Furthermore, our prayers ought to be frequent but short, lest, if they are prolonged, the enemy who seeks to attack us would have an opportunity to slip in some distraction. In such prayers we have true sacrifice: "The sacrifice that God wills is a contrite heart." There, too, we make the salutary oblation, the pure offering, the "sacrifice of justice," the "sacrifice of praise." There we have the burnt-offerings of fatlings, the offering of a contrite and humbled heart. If we present ourselves before God according to the method and with the fervor we have spoken of here, we shall be able to sing and know we are heard: "Let my prayer rise like incense before your face, the lifting of my hands like the evening offering."

Chapter Nine

Hearing the Message

In the preceding pages, we have been invited and challenged to listen to a number of the Church Fathers and Christian writers of the early centuries of the Christian era for a answer to the question which inspired this volume: WHAT DO THE FATHERS TELL US ABOUT PRAYER? In some instances, we seem to have strayed far afield, following modes and themes which may seem foreign to modern ears and contemporary *praxis.* It may even have happened that all the texts taken together have only served to sharpen our question. On the whole, the message has been constant, faithful to the Scriptures, concerned with probing and explicating the way in which our ancestors in the faith understood and sought to encourage God's coming to us and our going to him.

In this final section, a number of brief texts will be presented, in an attempt to provide a kaleidoscopic overview of the early Christian teaching on prayer. The selections, largely, will speak for themselves. They are not intended to be a twentieth-century *catena aurea* of sorts. Authors not cited earlier in this work appear in the following pages. The "definitions" of prayer and praying offered here are given by way of "recapitulation" of the entire volume.[41]

[41] *Sources, Les Mystiques Chrétiens des Origines,* Olivier Clement. Paris: Stock, 1982.

1. Prayer is a "conversation of the mind with God. Seek, then, the state the mind needs so that, without a backward glance, it may tend towards its Lord and converse with him, without any intermediary.

    Evagrius the Pontic *On Prayer*, 3 (PG 79.1168)

2. If it be true that the Divine principle is present in every being, every being on the contrary does not reside in the Divine principle. It is by invoking the Divinity through holy prayers, with a tranquil mind... that we also come to reside in Divinity. For this residence is not localized, so that it would be changed from place to place.... If we were on a boat and were thrown some ropes attached to a rock so as to be rescued, it is clear that we would not be drawing the rock to ourselves. Rather, we, and with us the boat, would be hauled in toward the rock.... And that is why... We must begin by prayer, not to draw toward ourselves that Power which is at one and the same time everywhere and nowhere, but to place ourselves in his hands and to be united to him.   Dionysius the Areopagite
    The Divine Names III, 1 (PG 3.680)

3. By prayer, I understand not that which is found only in the mouth, but that which springs up from the bottom of the heart. Indeed, just as trees with the deepest roots are not broken or uprooted by a violent storm,... so too, prayers that come from the depths of the heart, rooted there, ascend to heaven with confidence. They are not turned aside under attack from any distracting thought at all. That is why the psalm says, "Out of the depths I have cried to you, O Lord" (Psalm 129, 1).

    John Chrysostom
    On the Incomprehensibility of God,
    Fifth Discourse (SC 28, 2nd ed., 320)

4. Prayer is the daughter of meekness.... Prayer is the fruit of joy and gratitude.   Evagrius the Pontic
    On Prayer, 14-15 (PG 79.1169)

5. If you desire to pray, you need God who gives prayer to one who does pray.   Evagrius the Pontic
   On Prayer, 58 (PG 79.1180)

6. If you are a theologian, you will truly pray and, if you pray truly, you are a theologian.
   Evagrius the Pontic *On Prayer*, 60 (PG 79.1180)

7. When the Holy Spirit acts in the soul, that person sings psalms and prays, in total submission and meekness in the secret of her heart. This disposition is accompanied by interior tears and, then, by a sense of a certain kind of fullness that thirsts and craves silence.
   Diadochus of Photice
   Chapters on Spiritual Perfection, 73 (SC5, 3rd ed., 132)

8. The Lord resides in a fervent soul. He establishes it at his throne of glory. He presides and abides there. The prophet Ezechiel speaks of the four living creatures harnessed to the Lord's chariot. He says that they have countless eyes. In this, they are like the one who seeks God—what do I say?—like one pursued by God. Such a person becomes, as it were, nothing other than a living gaze fixed on God.   Pseudo-Macarius
   Homily 33 (PG 34.741)

9. One who prays participates in the prayer of God's Word who lives among those who know not the Word, who is absent from no one's prayer. The Word prays to the Father in union with the believer whose Mediator he is. Indeed, the Son of God is the high priest of our offerings and our advocate with the Father. He prays for those who pray; he pleads for those who plead.
   Origen *On Prayer*, 10 (PG 11.445)

10. The Hesychast (from *hesychia*: silence, peace, sweet delight of union with God) is one who seeks to contain the incorporeal in the corporal. . . . The Hesychast's cell is defined by the very limits of his own body. There he finds a dwelling-place for wisdom.
    John Climacus *The Sacred Ladder*
    27th Degree; 5, 10 (PG 88.1097)

11. They asked the *abba* Macarius, "How ought we to pray?" The ancient one answered, "There is no need to lose oneself in words. It is enough to stretch out one's hands and to say, 'Lord, as you will and as you know: have mercy.' If trial and struggle weigh you down, cry out, 'Lord Help!' The Lord knows what is best for you and he will have mercy on you."

Macarius the Egyptian
Apophthegm 16 (19) (PG 34.249)

12. [Anthony] called his two companions...and said to them, "Let your very breath be always *Christ*."

Athanasius of Alexandria
Vita Antonii, XCI (PG 26.969)

13. *Amma* (Mother) Syncletica says, "There are many who dwell on the mountain and act as if they live in the midst of the city's tumult; they doom themselves. It is possible in the midst of a crowd to be interiorly alone and, though living alone, to be interiorly invaded by the crowd."   Syncletica *Apophthegm*, 19.41

14. One of the Fathers who is a Christ-bearer tells us that prayer is the silence of the pure. For their thoughts are divine movements. The movements of the purified heart and mind are voice full of sweetness by which those persons never cease singing in secret to the hidden God.   Isaac the Syrian

Ascetical Treatises, 85

15. A certain man, I am told, on beholding the body of a particularly beautiful woman, was impelled to glorify the Creator. He would even be moved to tears in his love for God, at the sight. . . . A man who experiences such sentiments and affections in that circumstance is already risen. . . before the general resurrection.

John Climacus *The Sacred Ladder*
15th Degree (PG 88.892)

16. Beloved: The Lord is our mirror.
    Open your eyes,
    Look at him.
    Learn to recognize your own faces!
    Odes of Solomon, 13, ed. Charlesworth

17. Sadness is a heavy burden;
    Repugnance is insupportable;
    But tears in God's presence
    Are stronger than either of these.
    Evagrius the Pontic
    A Mirror for Nuns, 39 (TU 39.149)

18. If you are at home, pray and praise God at the third
    hour (nine o'clock). If you are somewhere else, pray to
    God in your heart for, at that hour, Christ was nailed to
    the cross.... Hippolytus
    Apostolic Tradition, 41 (SC11.126, ed. Botte)

19. Each time we bend the knee and rise again, we show by
    that action that sin has cast us down to the earth and
    that the love of Christ has called us back to heaven.
    Basil of Caesarea
    Treatise on the Holy Spirit, 27 (SC17.238)

20. I have stretched out my hands
    In offering to the Lord,
    Hands stretched out signify that;
    Hands stretched out when I am standing upright
    Mean: the wood has been raised.
    Alleluia!
    Odes of Solomon, 27

SELECTED BIBLIOGRAPHY

In addition to the patristic texts from which excerpts have been included in this volume, the following works are suggested for further reading:

Bouley, Allan, O.S.B. *From Freedom to Formula.* Studies in Christian Antiquity 21. Washington, D.C.: The Catholic University of America Press, 1981.

Bouyer, Louis. *The Spirituality of the New Testament and the Fathers* (trans., Mary P. Ryan). History of Christian Spirituality I. New York/Tournai/Paris/Rome: Desclée and Company, Inc., 1963.

Bradshaw, Paul F. *Daily Prayer in the Early Church.* London: Alcuin Club/SPCK, 1981.

Hamman, A., O.F.M. *La Prière II: Les trois premiers siècles.* Tournai (Belgium): Desclée et Cie, Editeurs, 1963.

Hamman, Gauthier A. *Early Christian Prayers* (trans., Walter Mitchell). Chicago: H. Regnery Co., 1961.

Jungmann, Josef A. *The Place of Christ in Liturgical Prayer* (trans., A. Peeler). Staten Island, New York: Alba House, 1965.

Jungmann, Joseph A. *Christian Prayer Through the Centuries* (trans., John Coyne, S.J.). New York/Ramsey/Toronto: Paulist Press, 1978.

Savon, Hervé. *The Church and Christian Prayer.* Saint Severin Series for Adult Christians III (English version, Geoffrey Stevens). Notre Dame, Indiana: Fides Publications, Inc., 1965.

Simpson, Robert L. *The Interpretation of Prayer in the Early Church.* Philadelphia: The Westminster Press, 1965.

Squire, Aelred, O.S.B. *Asking the Fathers.* New York: Paulist Press, 1973.

Index